STACK & CUT
Hexagon Quilts

Mix & Match 38 Kaleidoscope Blocks & 12 Quilt Settings

NEW
Serendipity Patterns

SARA NEPHEW and MARCI BAKER

Text and photography copyright © 2018 by Sara Nephew and Marci Baker

Photography and artwork copyright © 2018 by C&T Publishing, Inc.

Publisher: Amy Marson

Creative Director: Gailen Runge

Editor: Lynn Koolish

Technical Editor: Helen Frost

Cover/Book Designer: Page + Pixel

Production Coordinator: Tim Manibusan

Production Editor: Jennifer Warren

Illustrator: Linda Johnson

Photo Assistant: Mai Yong Vang

Instructional photography by Diane Pedersen and Mai Yong Vang of C&T Publishing, Inc., unless otherwise noted

Published by C&T Publishing, Inc., P.O. Box 1456, Lafayette, CA 94549

All rights reserved. No part of this work covered by the copyright hereon may be used in any form or reproduced by any means—graphic, electronic, or mechanical, including photocopying, recording, taping, or information storage and retrieval systems—without written permission from the publisher. The copyrights on individual artworks are retained by the artists as noted in *Stack & Cut Hexagon Quilts*. These designs may be used to make items for personal use only and may not be used for the purpose of personal profit. Items created to benefit nonprofit groups, or that will be publicly displayed, must be conspicuously labeled with the following credit: "Designs copyright ©2018 by Sara Nephew and Marci Baker from the book *Stack & Cut Hexagon Quilts* from C&T Publishing, Inc." Permission for all other purposes must be requested in writing from C&T Publishing, Inc.

Attention Copy Shops: Please note the following exception—publisher and author give permission to photocopy pages 124–127 for personal use only.

Attention Teachers: C&T Publishing, Inc., encourages you to use this book as a text for teaching. Contact us at 800-284-1114 or ctpub.com for lesson plans and information about the C&T Creative Troupe.

We take great care to ensure that the information included in our products is accurate and presented in good faith, but no warranty is provided, nor are results guaranteed. Having no control over the choices of materials or procedures used, neither the author nor C&T Publishing, Inc., shall have any liability to any person or entity with respect to any loss or damage caused directly or indirectly by the information contained in this book. For your convenience, we post an up-to-date listing of corrections on our website (ctpub.com). If a correction is not already noted, please contact our customer service department at ctinfo@ctpub.com or P.O. Box 1456, Lafayette, CA 94549.

Trademark (™) and registered trademark (®) names are used throughout this book. Rather than use the symbols with every occurrence of a trademark or registered trademark name, we are using the names only in the editorial fashion and to the benefit of the owner, with no intention of infringement.

Library of Congress Cataloging-in-Publication Data

Names: Nephew, Sara, author. | Baker, Marcia L., author.

Title: Stack & cut hexagon quilts : mix & match 38 kaleidoscope blocks & 12 quilt settings - new serendipity patterns / Sara Nephew and Marci Baker.

Other titles: Stack and cut hexagon quilts

Description: Lafayette, CA : C&T Publishing, Inc., 2018.

Identifiers: LCCN 2017040201 | ISBN 9781617454691 (soft cover)

Subjects: LCSH: Patchwork--Patterns. | Quilting--Patterns.

Classification: LCC TT835 .N4595 2018 | DDC 746.46/041--dc23

LC record available at https://lccn.loc.gov/2017040201

Dedication

To all the wonderful quilters I've met.
—*Sara*

In memory of Sue Bailey—my mentor, cheerleader,
and blessed friend.
—*Marci*

Acknowledgments

Thank you to all the quilters who made beautiful quilts for *Stack & Cut Hexagon Quilts*: Virginia L. Anderson, Laurie Biundo, Janet Blazekovich, Benita Cole, Joan Dawson, Linda Rose DeGaeta, Becky Dietz, Martha Ethridge, Cindy Fredrick, Diane Gilbreath, Cindy Glancy, Janice Jamison, Katie Kennedy, Kathie Kryla, Kate McIntyre, Romona Melnick, Elaine Muzichuk, Alicia B. Sanchez, Pamela Seaberg, Kathy Syring, and Pamela York. Each creation provides an added beauty to this book. Additionally, we thank you for your feedback on our instructions and your trust in us to present your works in their best light.

Thanks to Joan Dawson and Virginia L. Anderson for their helpful tips and suggestions.

Thank you to the following companies that provided supplies for several of these projects: In the Beginning Fabrics, Maywood Studio, Presencia America, Quilters Dream Batting, and YLI Threads. Your support of the art and craft of quilting with superior products makes our jobs and passion even more enjoyable.

Lastly, we are also indebted to our editors and all the staff at C&T Publishing who made this book possible. Having been self-published for many years, we both have an appreciation for the process. C&T Publishing's expertise takes our talents to a whole new level.

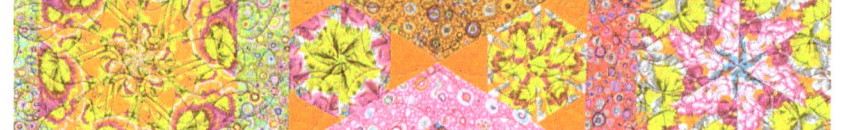

CONTENTS

Introduction 6

How to Use This Book 8

Tools 10
Cutting tools • Rulers

Plan Your Project 11

Selecting the Best Repeat Fabric 11
Choose a large print • Choose a high-contrast print • Get six repeats

Preparing the Stacked Repeat Fabric 15
Cut or tear the fabric repeats • Stack and align the repeats

Cutting the Strips 18
Design possibilities • Finding the best elements • Previewing your designs with mirrors • Cutting strips for supporting fabrics

Planning Your Design 22
Selecting the elements • Figuring yardage for supporting fabrics • Using multiple fabrics per shape

Sample Projects 24
Three-Block Table Runner • Eight-Block Quilt

BLOCK DESIGNS 32

 BADGE 34
 BEZEL 35
 BOLD STAR 36
 BUTTON 37
 CRYSTAL 38

 DAINTY 39
 DEW 40
 DUTCH STAR 41
 FLASHDANCE 42
 FLINT 43

 FROZEN 44
 KNOTTED CORD 45
 LAMP 46
 LITTLE GARDEN 47
 MAGIC 48

 MIX & MATCH 49
 MOONGLOW 50
 ORNAMENT 51
 PARK PLACE 52
 PATRIOT 53

 POINSETTIA 54
 PORTHOLE 55
 PRICKLY PEAR 56
 RINGSTONE 57
 RIPPLES 58

 ROSE WINDOW 59
 SAILOR'S DREAM 60
 SAILOR'S STAR 61
 SHY EYES 62
 SONATA 63

 STAINED GLASS 64
 STARRY PATH 65
 STARSTRUCK 66
 SUSAN 67
 TICKTOCK 68

 TIGERSTRIPE 69
 WAVING FLAGS 70
 WHIRLWIND 71

QUILT DESIGNS 72

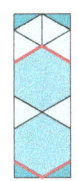 TWO-BLOCK DESIGN 73

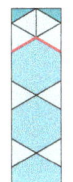 THREE-BLOCK DESIGN 74

 THREE-BLOCK DESIGN 1 (IN A LINE) 74

 THREE-BLOCK DESIGN 2 (IN THE ROUND) 74

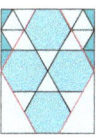 FOUR-BLOCK DESIGN 76

 FIVE-BLOCK DESIGN 77

 SIX-BLOCK DESIGN 78

 SEVEN-BLOCK DESIGN 79

 EIGHT-BLOCK DESIGN 86

 NINE-BLOCK DESIGN 87

 TEN-BLOCK DESIGN 94

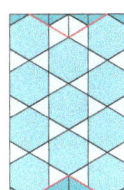 ELEVEN-BLOCK DESIGN 96

 OTHER QUILT DESIGNS 98

SETTING TRIANGLE DESIGNS 102

 SINGLE TRIANGLE 102

 CHESTNUT 103

 DARLING 104

 SERENDIPITY 105

SHAMROCK 106

SMILE 107

 STARBURST 108

BORDER DESIGNS 109

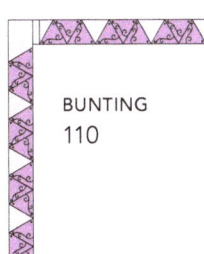 BUNTING 110

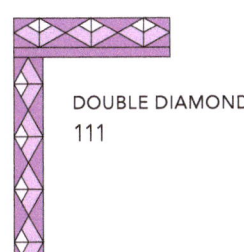 DOUBLE DIAMOND 111

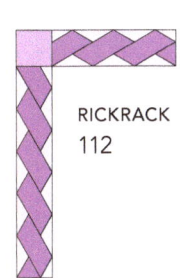 RICKRACK 112

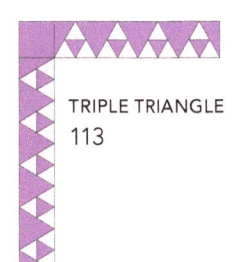 TRIPLE TRIANGLE 113

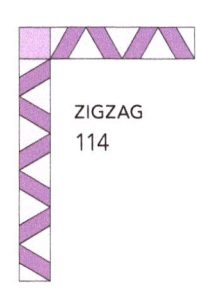 ZIGZAG 114

Cutting Shapes 115

Triangle halves • Triangles • Strip-pieced triangles • Diamonds • Long diamonds • Strip-pieced diamonds • Flat pyramids • Gems and hexagons • Matched triangles • Matched half-diamonds

Binding Other Angles 123

Patterns 124

About the Authors 128

INTRODUCTION

Search the internet for "The Three Princes of Serendip," and you will find an old fairy tale that emphasizes the usefulness of being *serendipitous*—watching for happy accidents you can benefit from because you are well prepared. Serendipity patterns show you how to use certain characteristics of printed fabrics to create new beauty and fun from simple kaleidoscope techniques. Stacking fabric layers with six repeats and cutting 60° shapes creates an all-new beauty.

Sara Nephew began these designs with her books *Serendipity Quilts* and *Doubledipity: More Serendipity Quilts*. In this book there are 38 new block designs, many with much larger center shapes. Use traditional large-scale prints or more modern prints with these larger shapes for new kaleidoscope designs. With popular prints being larger in scale, the possibilities open up for a lot of *wow!* factor. Marci observed that the block designs frame each fabric-created kaleidoscope in Sara's concept for these serendipitous quilts. Because the kaleidoscopes are separated, the viewer can appreciate the uniqueness of each and every one.

Ringstone by Joan Dawson (page 82)

Button by Janet Blazekovich (page 88)

tip

Sara has discovered that her fabric choices are becoming richer with detail as she makes more kaleidoscope quilts. The resulting quilts have more and more texture. After you have made your first stacked repeat quilt, you will find yourself looking at large prints in a whole new way. As you try another of these quilts, see if you grow toward working with more texture, as Sara has!

HOW TO USE THIS BOOK

We have designed *Stack & Cut Hexagon Quilts* so that you can collaborate with your fabric. Your choice of fabric allows you to design an incredible, individualized creation. Our methods for producing quilts are very different: Sara is an artist first, whereas Marci is an engineer by training. The way we view the world gives us very different ideas on the process.

With Sara's method, yardage is only needed for the large-print, high-contrast repeat fabric. All the supporting fabrics are chosen as the project progresses, and if one material is insufficient, another is picked.

Marci's process requires some decisions to be made in advance and yardages to be determined. If one fabric runs out, her method allows you to find a substitute—especially if it is available in your stash and means one less trip to the quilt shop! (That way you are less distracted from the current project.)

In this book, we've provided different elements for you to choose from so you can mix and match, combining them into your own creation. To get started, read Tools (page 10), Selecting the Best Repeat Fabric (page 11), Preparing the Stacked Repeat Fabric (page 15), Cutting the Strips (page 18), and Planning Your Design (page 22).

We've included two sample projects (Three-Block Table Runner and *Eight-Block Quilt*) that will show you how it all works. In both projects, we've explained what elements are chosen and how to figure yardage. You'll learn how to use the tables and diagrams provided with each block to gain confidence for your own project.

After you see how the process works, you are ready to choose the elements of your quilt—the block design (page 32), the quilt design (page 72), the setting triangles (page 102), and the borders (page 109)—and calculate your own yardage and cutting for the various elements.

Because there are so many variables, we leave it to you to figure out your backing, batting, and binding requirements. We highly recommend the *All-in-One Quilter's Reference Tool* (by C&T Publishing) to help with this.

For inspiration, we will show you quilts using each block, quilts with different block quantities, and quilts with a variety of borders (see Quilt Designs, page 72). Seven of the many possible pieced borders have been developed into specific piecing instructions.

Because the focus of this book is on the elements that make up the quilts, we have placed the cutting instructions for the shapes near the back of the book. The methods are simple, and you will probably find that you become familiar and comfortable enough that you do not need to refer to this section. One practice that our students have found helpful in the beginning is to place a sticky note on the project pages and another on the cutting instructions; as you are working, you can easily move back and forth in the book as needed.

Refer to the following sections to figure out yardage:

Figuring Yardage for Supporting Fabrics (page 22)

Using Multiple Fabrics per Shape (page 23)

Figuring Yardage for Setting Triangles (page 30)

Figuring Yardage for Pieced Borders (page 109)

COLLABORATION: ARTIST AND ENGINEER

The more you work with these fabrics, the more skillful you will become at using color and pattern to build your blocks and compose your quilt. Each person has their own approach, and each way has its rewards. Here is what we experienced:

We decided to collaborate on sewing *Knotted Cord* (below right). Marci brought the repeat fabric and a bunch of jewel tones. We were in Sara's sewing room, full of a wide variety of fabrics. Marci cut and pressed while Sara sewed. There was some discussion between us about which repeat design was the best to put in the center, what colors to use in the corner diamonds of the blocks, and so on.

Our goal was to make nine blocks because that was what the fabric allowed. Marci watched as Sara made one block and then put it up on the wall to study. Sara began to choose what colors might look best in the next block; she reversed values just to do something different. When we had a few blocks made, we agreed that the first block was sour in color. So Sara unpicked the corners, and we put in a fabric that we both agreed was better. When we had five blocks, three of them were basically blue, another was yellow, and another was red.

Marci exclaimed, "I see! We can have three blue, three red, and three yellow blocks, and we'll have our nine-block layout!"

"No," Sara said, "We will just keep picking colors for the next block, studying the possibilities as we go."

This is when we fully realized the differences in our techniques. We knew there were contrasts in our quilts and in our fabric choices (Sara works with red, and Marci works with green); however, we could now appreciate our individualized methods.

Marci likes to look ahead and plan for speed, getting her quilts done quickly and being able to write efficient directions with speed-piecing tricks included. Her mind enjoys this thought process. Sara likes to make one block at a time with a more painterly approach, putting a little bit of color here and a little bit there—maybe even reversing values sometimes. Her art training and years of quilting help her to be successful in this eclectic approach. Both of us use equally great methods, producing unique and varied quilts. We *both* enjoy what we do; we both produce beautiful quilts. *And* we have fun working together.

Knotted Cord by Sara Nephew and Marci Baker

TOOLS

The tools needed to rotary cut the patterns in this book are very basic. We list our favorite brands in parentheses following each item.

Cutting Tools

Rotary cutter (OLFA)   The 45mm size is the best for speed and safety.

Self-healing mat (OLFA)   Marci uses the blank side of the mat to eliminate conflict between 90° and 60° lines.

Rulers

6˝ × 12˝ ruler (Omnigrid or Creative Grids)   Do you want to gain confidence in knowing that a strip is guaranteed to be straight when working with this shorter, more controllable ruler? See Tip: *C is for Cut* (page 21).

6˝ × 24˝ ruler (Omnigrid or Creative Grids)

60° ruler (Clearview Triangle 60° Acrylic Ruler [8˝ or 10˝ size] *or* Clearview Triangle Super 60° Acrylic Ruler, both by C&T Publishing)   *Note:* We will refer to these throughout the book as the Clearview Triangle ruler and the Clearview Super 60° ruler.

Corner-trimming tool (Corner Cut 60—2-in-1 Sewing Tool by C&T Publishing) Trim the points of 60° shapes for accurate and efficient piecing.

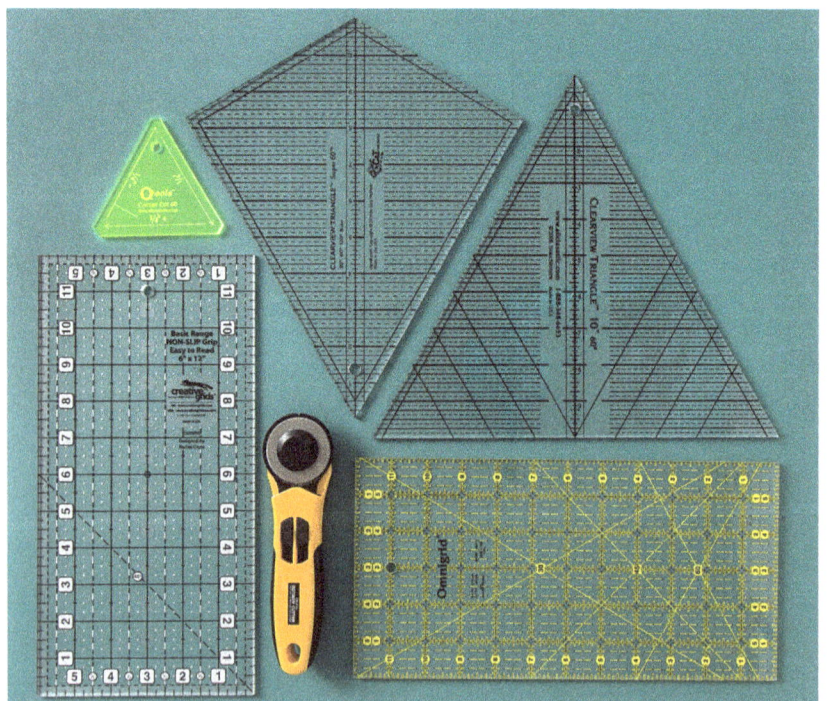

tip: Caution!
If you choose to use another manufacturer's 60° ruler, be sure to check your work as you go. The projects in this book were designed for the Clearview Triangle ruler or Clearview Super 60° ruler, so we highly recommend you use those. Other rulers, especially those with a flattened tip, can measure differently than what is illustrated here. The Clearview Triangle and Clearview Super 60° rulers are available from C&T Publishing (ctpub.com).

PLAN YOUR PROJECT

SELECTING THE BEST REPEAT FABRIC

For the quilts in this book you need 100% quilting-weight cotton (*no* flannels). In addition, there are a few more requirements.

Choose a Large Print

Be sure to choose a large print, not a fabric with tiny motifs sprinkled all over. (Save that for an accent fabric.) Think more of a Hawaiian print. The perfect fabric for stacking might make you say, "That is the ugliest fabric I have ever seen!" If not ugly, the print will surely be loud. It might be light and dark with just one color and a background.

Detail of *Park Place* (page 52)

With more colors in the print, you have more possibilities for accent fabrics. And with more colors and a very large print, the resulting blocks are quite varied and surprising.

Detail of *Jungle Fever* (page 84): An excellent choice of a very large print. Inset: Repeat fabric for *Jungle Fever*.

Plan Your Project 11

Detail of *Prickly Pear* (page 56): This large print provides myriad possibilities. Inset: Repeat fabric for *Prickly Pear*.

Preview Your Shapes

Check to see if the fabric being considered is a good selection by using the Clearview Triangle or Clearview Super 60° ruler to visualize the repeat shape. You can also make a copy of the template for that shape and make a viewing window out of paper or cardboard. Be sure that your templates are ¼″ smaller on all edges to allow for seam allowances; this will show you the repeat shape after the fabric has been sewn into the block. Because you will be cutting shapes from different areas of the fabric, each block will be different—so you have a number of opportunities to create spectacular blocks. See Cutting the Strips (page 18) for more information on how the fabric designs affect the look of the blocks.

tip

If you want to learn more about other types of stacked pattern repeats, read one of Maxine Rosenthal's books: *One-Block Wonders, One-Block Wonders Encore!,* or *One-Block Wonders Cubed!* (all by C&T Publishing).

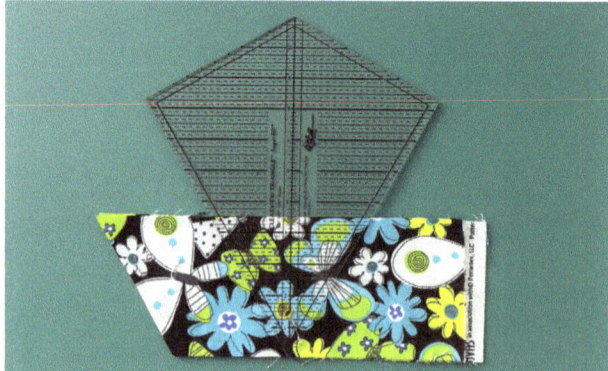

Large 6¼″ Clearview Super 60° triangle viewing window with repeat fabric

Large 6¼″ paper triangle viewing window with repeat fabric

Medium 3½″ paper triangle viewing window with the same repeat fabric

If the elements of the fabric fall into portions of the repeat shape as they do in both the large triangle and the medium triangle, then the fabric is a good choice. However, if there are no distinct elements in the window or under the ruler, then the print is either too small or too large.

Choose a High-Contrast Print

Be sure that the large print you've selected is high contrast. This means there will be some areas that are very dark and some that are very light, perhaps with a hard, sharp edge between the two. High-contrast prints help create unexpected shapes when stacked and cut. When the design elements fade from one to the other, the overall effect is less than stunning.

This fabric is a poor choice because it is low contrast with few strong lines.

tip

Take time to choose the right pattern for the fabric or the right fabric for the pattern. When you are gripped by the excitement of diving into a new project, slow down a bit and think about the quilt you want to make. Use the rulers and/or cut-out templates (see Preview Your Shapes, page 12) to determine if the size of the triangle or diamond in the block design fits the print size of the repeat fabric. If it works, go for it. If it doesn't fit, find another fabric or pick another block design.

Detail of *Button* (page 88): This large high-contrast print is a great choice. Inset: Repeat fabric for *Button*.

Get Six Repeats

It helps to imagine the fabric being printed off a roller. One complete turn of the roller creates one repeat panel of the design. To recognize this, look along the selvage edge of the fabric for an easy-to-notice detail—maybe a particular flower, the curve of a line, or a spot. Consider this as zero. Look along the selvage edge until you see that detail again; then count one for the first repeat. Measure this distance, and make note of the repeat length. Keep looking along the same edge till you see it again; then count two. Find up to the sixth repeat, and mark this point with a pin. Count again to verify that there are six repeats. The yardage to buy is this amount plus a little extra (⅛–¼ yard), to give you room to choose the best spot for your first cut. If the repeat fabric is to be used for the border, have a second piece cut and labeled as the border. This ensures the right yardage is used for the appropriate part of the quilt.

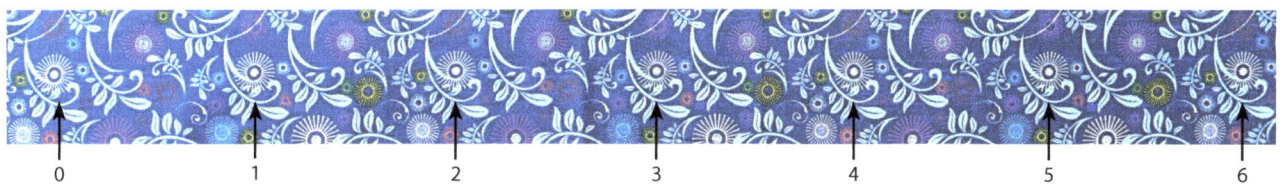

Counting zero through six of a specific design element—the white starburst—for six repeats of the design

Plan Your Project 13

The minimum yardage requirement for 9 blocks plus 24 setting triangles has been determined with each block design. The repeat length is given as a minimum (for example, 18″) so that all these shapes can be cut with minimal extra fabric. Note that some repeats are very short—even 6″, which might be an indicator that the print is too small. If the repeat is 12″ and you need 18″ for your project, use 2 repeats for every cut panel. This means you will need to purchase 12 repeats.

Be warned that you might run into a fabric design that will fool you. You look for a motif along the edge and you find it; then you look again and find that the first repeat is not *exactly* the same. Often what surrounds a "repeat" of this kind isn't the same, or it's not the same distance from the edge. When you figure out the actual repeat, the yardage is significantly different. Be alert! Prevent another trip to the store to buy more fabric.

Let's look back at the fabric shown for counting six repeats (page 13), now in full view. It is actually only three repeats. Notice that to the right of and just above the starburst the pattern alternates between a blue dot and no blue dot. (If you saw this in the first photograph, you are looking for all the right details. Just remember to start with zero and count to six.) So when you find a design element along the edge—especially if the distance between the repeated elements is less than 12″ or so—look further in from the edge of the fabric to be sure the repeat is as expected.

If the size of the repeat is significantly larger than the size the block needs, you will have fabric left over. You may be asking, "Am I going to end up with a closet full of leftover prints?" There are ways to use these leftovers: Members in your guild might appreciate being able to buy a length of fabric for their own kaleidoscope quilts. Or you could incorporate the panel into the borders or the back of the quilt. In fact, it is a good idea to put part of the repeat fabric on the quilt back. People are constantly surprised by the repeats produced when you show the original fabric to them.

tip

There may be times when helpful quilt shop workers, fabric manufacturers, or even yourself have done quick math and estimated yardage, only to find that there are only four or five repeats when you begin your project at home. Not buying enough fabric to start with is actually wasteful of fabric. While at the store, be sure to count the repeated motif (zero through six) a second time. Measure and count twice; cut once!

tip

Watch out for unexpected surprises. Though you have chosen a theme fabric, like toys or cute bugs, cutting them apart and assembling a new design might impart an entirely different feeling to the quilt, determined by the underlying shapes and colors you are working with. One of my bigger concerns is that I don't like body parts (or what I perceive to be a body part) as part of my design. For example, I once had a circle of realistic-looking ears appear that actually were part of an apple slice in the original fabric design. Avoid this by previewing your designs (page 12).

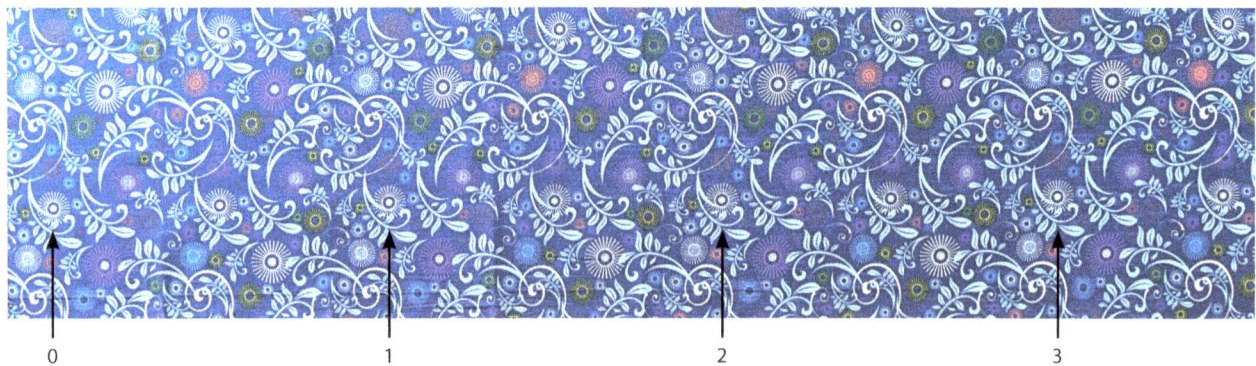

Counting zero through three of a specific design element—the white starburst with a blue dot above and to the right

PREPARING THE STACKED REPEAT FABRIC

Sara prefers to wash, dry, and press the fabric selvage to selvage. Her method of washing—a light soaking in plain water and then pressing on a flannel surface with a light hand (to be sure the design does not stretch)—works well for this technique. Marci does not prewash, and therefore the fabric is straight off the bolt.

Cut or Tear the Fabric Repeats

1. With the fabric folded in half selvage to selvage, make a notch at the fold and tear the fabric in half lengthwise. This gives you 2 easy-to-handle lengths of at least 6 design repeats each. If the yardage matches the minimum requirement for the project, both lengths will be used. Otherwise the second half can be used for backing, used for another project, or shared with a friend.

2. Along the selvage or the inside torn edge, near one cut end, find a memory point (a particular detail, such as a leaf or seashell) that will make it easy to see the 6 repeats. Find the next occurrence of this detail along the same long edge, being sure there is 1 whole repeat between this and the previous occurrence (see Get Six Repeats, page 13).

3a. Sara places a 6″ × 24″ clear ruler across the width of the fabric section at this memory point. Finding 2 or 3 more reference points across the width of the fabric, she lines up the ruler perpendicular to the selvage edge. Keeping the reference points in mind and finding them again each time, she cuts 6 repeats with a rotary cutter. This makes 6 identical panels from the original length of fabric.

Finding reference points for six identical repeats

3b. Marci snips the edge at each memory point and then rips across the fabric to save time and eliminate the need for a 24″-long ruler. This means that there will be a little more fabric trimmed off the edges and that the strips will be cut with the crosswise grain rather than the lengthwise grain. To reduce the amount of thread unraveling at the edges, she clips the corners at a diagonal. The threads will not be connected and therefore will stop raveling.

Sara says that she has seen fabrics where tearing was not successful. Marci's only experience with designs not lining up was when a student purchased her fabric from a big box store. It would not have mattered if it was torn or rotary cut—it was printed such that the design was printed unevenly across the fabric.

Stack and Align the Repeats

Place six repeat sections on top of each other. Count the layers to make sure you have six. The goal is to align specific points from layer to layer and to affix the layers so they do not shift. When the shapes are cut, all six should be the same printed motif. The selected points for aligning need to be precise small details in the printed element, such as the tip of a line, the V at a junction of a leaf and flower, a dot, or other similar point. Many of the methods shown for keeping the layers together use flat-head pins. Sara and Marci have each come up with their own methods using needle and thread: one with stitches, the other using knots. With either method you can easily align points and avoid nicking the rotary cutter blade or rocking the ruler over the thickness of pins.

Sara's Method of Aligning the Repeats

Use a regular sewing needle with double thread and a large knot at the end.

1. With the fabric layers stacked and somewhat aligned, rest your hand on top of one end of the stack. Put the point of the needle in a detail near the center of the panel on the first layer; then pull the layer up onto the needle, flipping the excess over your hand.

2. Repeat with the second layer, keeping the needle in the same position. Only move slightly as necessary to precisely pierce the same detail.

3. When the needle is through all 6 layers, run the needle back through the layers right next to the original piercing, pulling the knot tight. Make this stitch as small as possible.

4. Make several backstitches from this point by putting the needle front to back and then back to front. These are very small stitches that will keep the initial stitch in place.

5. Do this over the whole stack, putting a stitch or knot every 4″ in all directions. During this process, shake and smooth the whole stack as necessary to make the layers lie flat.

6. When the tacking is finished, touch with an iron here and there to mesh the layers together.

Marci's Method of Aligning the Repeats

Select perle cotton thread and a corresponding needle with a sharp point (not one used for cross-stitch or needlepoint); Marci prefers a long doll needle. Thread the needle with a single strand. Make a very large knot at the end that will not pull through the fabric. The knot should be the kind you learned early in sewing: Loop around the finger, roll along the finger to the end, and then pull tight. Messy is good.

1. Align the designs on the layers fairly closely. Starting with the top layer, put the needle in at a chosen detail in the center of the panel. Pull the layer up onto the needle, and then put the needle into the same point on the second layer.

2. Continue until all 6 layers are on the needle. Pull the needle to the back so the knot is tight against the top layer.

3. With the stack upside down, shift the layers around the knot until the knot underneath is directly below the point where the thread exits the fabric.

4. Bring the needle through a loop of thread to make a knot as close to the fabric as possible.

5. Continue adding to this knot in the same way, with the new knot being created below the first. After 3 or 4 of these simple knots, the entire knot will be large enough to not come through the fabric.

6. Do this over the whole stack, putting a stitch or knot every 4″ in all directions. During this process, shake and smooth the whole stack as necessary to make the layers lie flat.

7. When the tacking is finished, touch with an iron here and there to mesh the layers together.

CUTTING THE STRIPS

Now that the fabric is stacked, the repeat shapes are ready to be cut. Realizing how different elements in the fabric design yield different results in the block allows you to make the resulting quilt even more spectacular. From our experience, certain design elements provide a more desired look. As you cut your shapes, keep in mind how the elements affect the look of the resulting blocks. Preview your shapes (page 12) to get a better idea of how to cut the fabric. Triangles and diamonds are shown; gem shapes and flat pyramids have effects similar to diamonds.

By seeing the general variations that can happen, you can get an idea of what to expect. If you know you like the look of the designs shown here, then look for elements in the fabric where you can cut the appropriate shape. The little white circle in the following illustrations shows how the shapes have been rotated within the block.

This information has been provided to guide you as you begin your journey of stacked repeat quilts; however, we don't recommend overthinking this part—this is where the magic happens and the fabric sings!

Refer to Cutting Shapes (page 115) for instructions on how to cut out each type of shape.

Design Possibilities

The following illustrations show what happens when shapes are put together and when the individual shapes are rotated. To get an idea of what design elements are available in your stacked fabrics, you can preview your shapes (page 12) using a ruler or cut-out paper or cardboard windows.

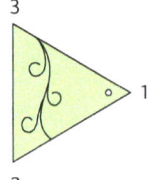

Triangle with the design element along one side

Rotate the triangle to see the variations.

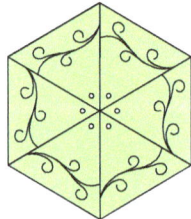

Design element on the outside edge of the block

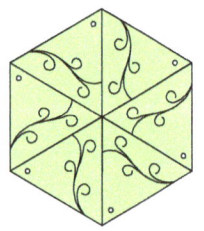

Design element rotated to appear on the inside edge

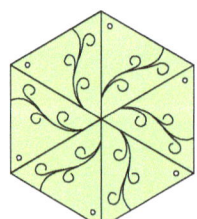

Design element rotated to appear on the other inside edge; a different central design appears.

FINDING THE BEST ELEMENTS

Here's another area where Sara and Marci take a somewhat different approach.

Marci tends to simply cut her stacked repeat fabric into the needed strip widths and take the results as they come.

Sara, taking a tip from Virginia L. Anderson (who has made a number of serendipity quilts), takes the time to think about her stacked fabric. She often places her main fabric on the floor after she has cut the repeats. While watching television she glances at the material, appreciating and getting to know the shapes and designs scattered across the weave. In one case, Sara realized that she had begun cutting repeats in such a way that she was basically eliminating one of her favorite motifs. So she set this first stack aside and cut repeat shapes from the other lengthwise half. Now she had beautiful blocks from her favorite part of the fabric.

The lesson is that you can fussy cut your strips and shapes to some extent, shifting things this way or that. Just keep in mind that if you only have just enough fabric, you may not be able to do this shifting.

tip

We suggest you read the next chapter, Planning Your Design (page 22), before you start cutting.

Triangle with the element going from side to side

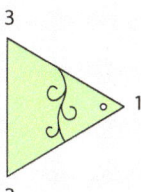

Triangle with the design element going through the center of the triangle from the base to the point

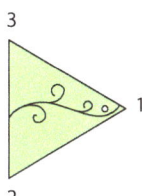

Diamond with the design element at one end

Diamond with the design element at one side

Diamond with the design element from point to point

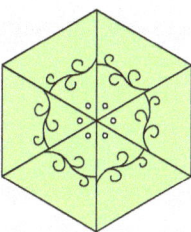

Design element going through the center of the block

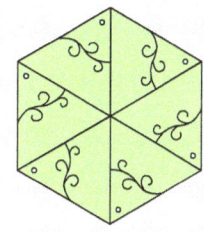

Design element going from the outside edge of the block to the interior seam

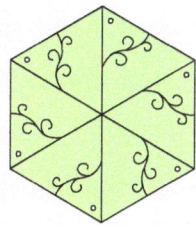

Design element going from the outside edge of the block to the other interior seam

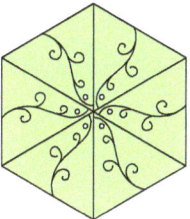

Design element going from the outside edge of the block to the center

Design element going from the outside corner of the block to the interior seam

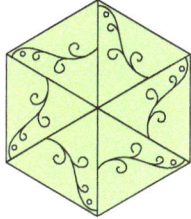

Design element going from the other outside corner of the block to the other interior seam

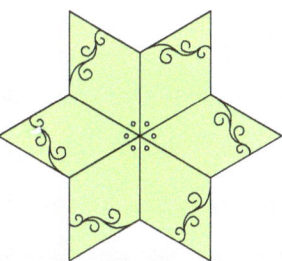

Design element at the outside points

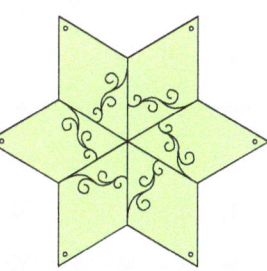

Design element at the inside points

Design elements at one corner

Design elements at the other corner

Design elements going from the points to the center

Design elements reversed for a different look

Plan Your Project 19

Previewing Your Designs with Mirrors

Use two small mirrors taped together so they open like a book. Open the mirrors to 60° using the Clearview Super 60° or Clearview Triangle ruler, and tape or glue a thread in position so it won't open farther. Set this opened mirror book on the fabric for a preview of the designs you will get from sets of stacked fabric. This is not the final design because every other section is reversed, which does not happen with the actual fabric. But if you don't like surprises, this might be the method for you.

Cutting Strips for Supporting Fabrics

This rotary cutting method allows fabric strips to be cut easily and successfully, and you'll know before you cut that the strip will be straight. The end of the fabric is cut, and more strips are cut without turning the larger piece of fabric.

1. Fold your fabric selvage to selvage. Slide the selvages left or right until they are parallel and there are no wrinkles in the fabric. Press or smooth out the layers.

2. Fold the fabric again, with the first fold pulled up just over the selvage. Press or smooth out the layers.

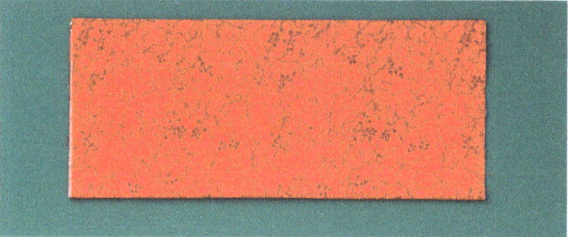

3. From the *left end* of the fabric, use the 6″ × 12″ ruler to measure that the folds are parallel. If they are not parallel, one side of fabric will be longer than the other. To fix this, lift and move the top single-fold slightly toward the end that is longer. Adjust until both folds are parallel.

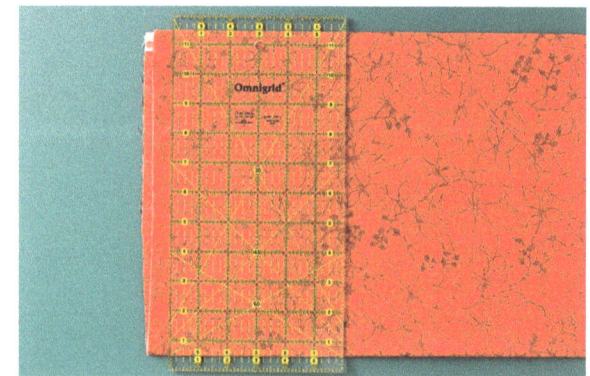

20   STACK & CUT Hexagon Quilts

4. At the left end of the fabric, align the ruler so that it is parallel to the top and bottom folds and covers the strip width and any fabric that needs to be trimmed. Cut on the ruler's right edge.

5. Turn the small cut piece 180°. Align the ruler with the top and bottom folds and with the cut width along the left edge. Trim off the scrap on the ruler's right edge.

6. Continue aligning the ruler with the folds and straight edge and cutting strips from the remaining fabric until you have the required number of strips. If the top fold, the edge measurement, and the bottom fold do not all line up, repeat Steps 3–5 to refold and trim the fabric to be square.

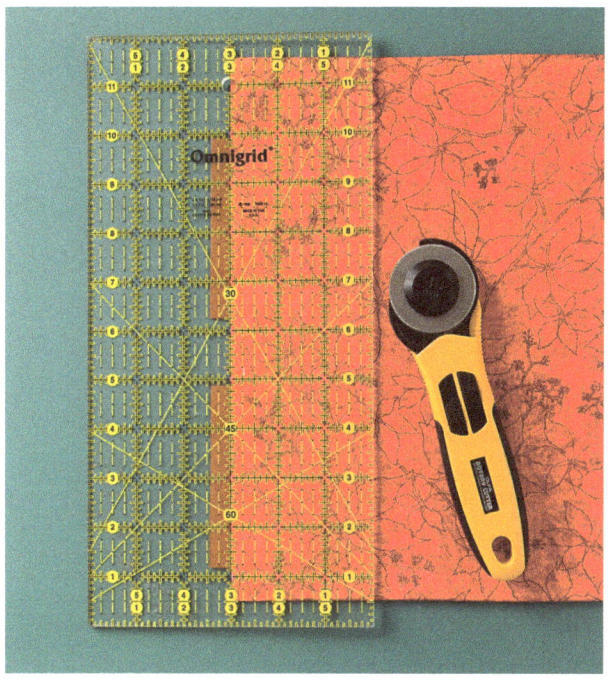

tip: C Is for Cut

Because this is different than how most of our students cut, we teach them this hint to remember: "C is for cut—look for the C when aligning the ruler." The C is the alignment of the ruler at the top fold, along the ruler line for the strip width, and at the bottom of the fold. If there is not a C, then it is time to realign the fabric so that the folds are parallel.

PLANNING YOUR DESIGN

Selecting the Elements

Each kaleidoscope quilt has four basic elements built around a repeat fabric:

Block design: Determines which block to piece
Quilt design: Determines how many blocks to make
Setting triangles: Connects the blocks
Borders (pieced or not pieced): Finishes the quilt

Each block design can be placed in any quilt design. Any setting triangle can be used with any block or any setting. With this mix-and-match approach, yardages are added together rather than given as a total.

Block Design

To select a block design (page 32), consider what your repeat fabric looks like. Use the Clearview Triangle ruler, Clearview Super 60° ruler, or a template window (page 12) to determine the best shape and size (see Previewing Your Designs with Mirrors, page 20).

Quilt Design

Select the quilt design (page 72), taking into consideration the number of blocks possible from the amount of repeat fabric available and their arrangement.

Setting Triangles

We recommend deciding on the setting triangles (page 102) *after* the blocks are made. To see them in action, refer to the quilts listed with each design.

Borders

Pieced borders (page 109) or plain borders can be added to finish (and enlarge) a quilt. Pieced borders are often selected after the center of the quilt is made.

Figuring Yardage for Supporting Fabrics

Each of the block designs includes a table with fabric requirements and cutting for nine blocks (sometimes less). Nine is the most common number of blocks for the quilts in this book and for the supporting yardage—the lights, mediums, and darks for the rest of the block. For example, see the table below.

FABRIC	YARDAGE FOR 9 BLOCKS	STRIP QUANTITY AND SIZE TO CUT FOR 9 BLOCKS	QUANTITY, SHAPE, AND SIZE TO CUT FOR 9 BLOCKS	QUANTITY OF SHAPE IN 1 BLOCK
REPEAT (R) (A set is 6 layers.)	Minimum of 18″ repeat or 3 yards	3 sets of stacked strip sets 4⅝″ × 20″	9 triangle sets 4⅝″ (page 116)	1 set of 6
LIGHT (L)	½ yard	4 strips 2⅛″ × WOF	108 triangles 2⅛″ (page 116)	12
MEDIUM (M)	½ yard	3 strips 3½″ × WOF	54 triangles 3½″ (page 116)	6
DARK (D)	1¼ yards	11 strips 3¼″ × WOF	108 diamonds 3¼″ (page 117)	12

From this information, it is easy to determine yardage for the repeat fabric and the supporting fabrics for a different number of blocks. In the example below, we will determine the yardage for a five-block quilt design. The calculations are easy to do on a basic calculator. As needed, convert the fractions to decimals using Conversion Chart—Fractions to Decimals.

Conversion Chart—Fractions to Decimals

FRACTION	⅛	¼	⅜	½	⅝	¾	⅞
DECIMAL	.125	.25	.375	.5	.625	.75	.875

Conversion Chart—Inches to Yards

INCHES	4.25″	9″	13.5″	18″	22.5″	27″	31.5″
YARDS	⅛	¼	⅜	½	⅝	¾	⅞
INCHES	36″	40.5″	45″	49.5″	54″		
YARDS	1	1⅛	1¼	1⅜	1½		

Step 1: Figure the number of inches needed for each fabric for 9 blocks using the chart.

Refer to the third column: strip quantity and size to cut for 9 blocks. For each fabric listed other than the repeat fabric, multiply the strip quantity to cut by the strip size to cut.

Light: 4 × 2.125″ = 8.5″
Medium: 3 × 3.5″ = 10.5″
Dark: 11 × 3.25″ = 35.75″

Step 2: Figure the amount needed for 5 blocks.

Divide the number from Step 1 by 9 to get the number of inches per block. Then multiply by 5 for 5 blocks. Round up to nearest ¼″ for simplicity.

Light: 8.5″ ÷ 9 = .94″
   .94″ × 5 = 4.72″ (*Round up to 4.75″.*)

Medium: 10.5″ ÷ 9 = 1.17″
   1.17″ × 5 = 5.85″ (*Round up to 6″.*)

Dark: 35.75″ ÷ 9 = 3.97″ (*Round up to 4″.*)
   4″ × 5 = 20″

Step 3: Add in an extra strip width and 3″ for fabric straightening for good measure.

Light: 4.75″ + 2.125″ + 3″ = 9.875″
Medium: 6″ + 3.5″ + 3″ = 12.5″
Dark: 20″ + 3.25″ + 3″ = 26.25″

Step 4: Convert inches to yards, rounding up to the nearest ⅛ yard.

Use the conversion chart (at left) if needed.

Light: 9.875″ rounds up to ⅜ yard.
Medium: 12.5″ rounds up to ⅜ yard.
Dark: 26.25″ rounds up to ¾ yard.

Using Multiple Fabrics per Shape

The yardage given for the block design is for nine blocks made from the same fabrics. By adding in more variety, the quilt rises to a whole new level. Here is any easy way to collect the fabrics:

If the strip is less than 4″, then ⅛ yard will be sufficient. Get an ⅛ yard for each block being made plus an extra ⅛ yard for any cutting mistakes.

If the shape requires a strip 4″ or wider, then ¼ yard per block will suffice. However, if there are more than 9 strips required for a particular shape, then you will need ⅜ yard per block for that shape.

tips

- To make a beautiful quilt with a colorful, well-balanced design, you will generally need a variety of fabrics. When purchasing the accent fabrics, use the table shown for your chosen block to determine the required yardage to buy. As you are making the blocks and setting triangles, a fabric's value or color may not seem to fit. Be willing to try new fabrics to refresh the color scheme or to balance the weight of the pattern.

- To make selecting accent fabrics at the quilt shop easier, iron the first repeat set onto freezer paper or wax paper (or baste it together) and take this with you to the store.

SAMPLE PROJECTS

Three-Block Table Runner

FINISHED TABLE RUNNER: 24½″ × 65″

Starry Path block

Butterflies in My Garden by Diana Gilbreath

This is a perfect project size for a class or for those wanting to try out the techniques. Because the repeat-fabric requirements are more than are needed in this design, sharing with a friend or two is advantageous. Use the second length of fabric for the backing and/or borders. This can be a small project that then leads to a larger quilt with the same repeat fabric!

To make it easier for you to get started, we've provided all the yardage and cutting information—you don't need to do any calculations yourself.

Making the Starry Path Blocks

YARDAGE AND CUTTING FOR STARRY PATH BLOCKS

Cut the strips and corresponding shapes using the instructions on the pages noted in the table.

FABRIC	YDG FOR 3 BLOCKS	STRIP QTY AND SIZE TO CUT FOR 3 BLOCKS	QTY, SHAPE, AND SIZE TO CUT FOR 3 BLOCKS	QTY OF SHAPE IN 1 BLOCK
REPEAT (R) (A set is 6 layers.)	Min. of 12″ repeat or 2 yards	1 stacked strip set 3½″ × 20″	3 triangle sets 3½″ (page 116)	1 set of 6
LIGHT 1 (L1)	¼ yard	1 strip 3½″ × WOF	18 triangles 3½″ (page 116)	6
LIGHT 2 (L2) (Includes setting triangle and end pieces)	⅝ yard	1 strip 3½″ × WOF	18 triangles 3½″ (page 116)	6
MEDIUM (M)	⅜ yard	2 strips 3½″ × WOF	36 triangles 3½″ (page 116)	12
DARK (D)	⅝ yard	4 strips 3¼″ × WOF	36 diamonds 3¼″ (page 117)	12

24 STACK & CUT Hexagon Quilts

PIECING

Review General Information for Making Blocks (page 32). Seam allowances are ¼" unless otherwise noted. Follow the arrows for pressing directions.

Starry Path block

1. Determine the best selection of a 3½" repeat-fabric triangle set (see Cutting the Strips, page 18). After the shapes are cut, refer to Design Possibilities (page 18) for ideas on how the shapes can be rotated for different looks. When you've determined the best look for each set of shapes, mark the center so you can piece them together appropriately.

2. Using 1 repeat-fabric triangle, 1 L1 triangle, 1 L2 triangle, 2 M triangles, and 2 D diamonds, arrange 1 wedge.

3. Sew 2 M triangles on either side of the L1 triangle. Attach the repeat-fabric triangle to make the upper unit.

4. Sew 2 D diamonds on either side of the L2 triangle to make the lower unit.

5. Join the upper and lower units to complete 1 wedge.

6. Make 6 identical wedges, pressing the seam between the units up for 3 wedges and down for 3 wedges.

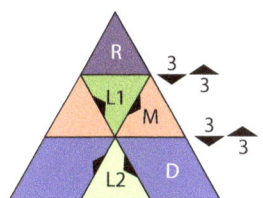

Starry Path wedge

7. Arrange the wedges into a hexagon, with the repeat fabric at the center. Alternate the direction of the seam between the units.

8. Sew the wedges into groups of 3 to make half-hexagons. Then sew the center seam to complete the block. Refer to Sewing and Pressing Options (page 32) as needed.

Making the Serendipity Setting Triangles

This quilt has solid fabric with machine embroidery for the setting triangles. This is a wonderful option and makes use of the beautiful embroidery designs available today. We have included the Serendipity setting triangle for a similar effect and to utilize the remaining stacked repeat fabric.

YARDAGE AND CUTTING FOR SERENDIPITY SETTING TRIANGLES

Cut the strips and corresponding shapes using the instructions on the pages noted in the table.

FABRIC	YDG FOR 4 SETTING TRIANGLES	STRIP QTY AND SIZE TO CUT FOR 4 SETTING TRIANGLES	QTY, SHAPE, AND SIZE TO CUT FOR 4 SETTING TRIANGLES	QTY OF SHAPE IN 1 SETTING TRIANGLE
REPEAT (R)	Included in block design (no additional fabric needed)	Use remainder of stacked strip set 3½" × 20".	4 triangle sets 3½" (page 116)	1 set of 6
LIGHT (L2)	Included in block design (no additional fabric needed)	1 strip 3½" × WOF	12 triangles 3½" (page 116)	3

Three-Block Table Runner

Setting Triangle Cutting and Piecing

Seam allowances are ¼" unless otherwise noted. Follow the arrows for pressing directions.

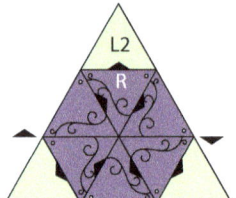

Serendipity setting triangle piecing

1. Determine the best selection of a 3½" repeat-fabric triangle set (see Cutting the Strips, page 18). After the shapes are cut, refer to Design Possibilities (page 18) for ideas on how the shapes can be rotated for different looks. Mark the center so you can piece them together appropriately.

2. Using 1 repeat-fabric triangle set and 3 L2 triangles, arrange 1 setting triangle.

3. Sew the repeats into 2 groups of 3 to make half-hexagons. Sew the center seam to complete the hexagon. Refer to Sewing and Pressing Options (page 32) as needed.

4. Add 3 L2 triangles on alternating corners.

5. Make 4 setting triangles.

Quilt Design

YARDAGE AND CUTTING FOR QUILT ASSEMBLY

FABRIC	YDG	STRIP QTY AND SIZE TO CUT	QTY, SHAPE, AND SIZE TO CUT
LIGHT (L2) for end pieces	Included in block design (no additional fabric needed)	1 strip 5½", subcut into 2 rectangles 5½" × 9½"	2 L and 2 R triangles halves (page 115)
BORDER 1	⅜ yard	4 strips 1½" × WOF	
BORDER 2	Use second length of repeat fabric.	6 strips 3½" × WOF	
BINDING	½ yard	5 strips your favorite size	
BATTING	32½" × 73"		
BACKING	2⅛ yards		

QUILT ASSEMBLY

1. Arrange the blocks, setting triangles, and end pieces as shown in the assembly diagram.

2. Sew each block and its corresponding triangles/end pieces to create diamond and partial diamond units.

3. Join the central diamond units and end pieces to complete the center of the runner.

4. Add the borders, layer the pieced top with the batting and backing, quilt, and bind.

We hope you have found the joy of working with these beautiful large-print fabrics. This is just the beginning!

Three-Block Table Runner assembly

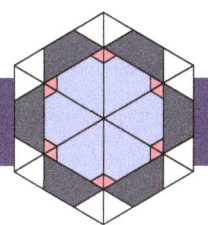

Eight-Block Quilt

FINISHED QUILT: 65½″ × 73″
Knotted Cord block

When creating the yardage and cutting charts for all the blocks in this book, we used nine blocks per quilt as the baseline. Because not all quilts have nine blocks, this sample project is another example of how to determine yardages for the number of blocks you are making.

Also covered in this sample project is how to determine yardages needed for a shape using multiple fabrics, as that is how we made the quilt. The block design used is Knotted Cord (page 45), and the setting triangle design is Chestnut (page 103). End pieces and simple borders were added to complete the quilt.

Knotted Cord by Sara Nephew and Marci Baker

Figuring Supporting Fabric Yardage for Just Eight Blocks

Using the original Knotted Cord yardage and cutting chart for nine blocks, determine the changes in yardage for eight blocks.

YARDAGE AND CUTTING FOR NINE BLOCKS

FABRIC	YDG FOR 9 BLOCKS	STRIP QTY AND SIZE TO CUT FOR 9 BLOCKS	QTY, SHAPE, AND SIZE TO CUT FOR 9 BLOCKS	QTY OF SHAPE IN 1 BLOCK
REPEAT (R) (A set is 6 layers.)	Minimum of 20″ repeat or 3½ yards	3 stacked strip sets 4⅝″ × 20″	9 diamond sets 4⅝″ (page 117)	1 set of 6
LIGHT (L)	¾ yard	6 strips 3½″ × WOF	108 triangles 3½″ (page 116)	12
MEDIUM (M)	½ yard	4 strips 2⅛″ × WOF	108 triangles 2⅛″ (page 116)	12
DARK (D)	1 yard	8 strips 3¼″ × WOF	54 flat pyramids 6¼″ (page 121)	6

REPEAT FABRIC FOR EIGHT BLOCKS

Because the block construction is based on stacking 6 layers of fabrics for the blocks, the yardage for the repeat fabric remains the same for 9 blocks or fewer. *However*, because the repeat yardage includes 24 Serendipity setting triangles and this project uses other fabrics, the repeat can be reduced by 7″ (the size we use to account for the setting triangle strips). So the minimum repeat can be 14″, which equates to a minimum of 2½ yards for 6 repeats.

SUPPORTING FABRICS FOR EIGHT BLOCKS

Refer to Conversion Chart—Fractions to Decimals and Conversion Chart—Inches to Yards (page 23) as needed.

Step 1: Figure the number of inches needed for each fabric for 9 blocks using the chart.

Refer to the third column: strip quantity and size to cut for 9 blocks. For each fabric listed other than the repeat fabric, multiply the strip quantity by the strip size.

Light: 6 × 3.50″ = 21″
Medium: 4 × 2.125″ = 8.5″
Dark: 8 × 3.25″ = 26″

Step 2: Figure the amount needed for 8 blocks.

Divide the number from Step 1 by 9 to get the number of inches per block. Then multiply by 8 for 8 blocks. Round up to nearest ¼″ for simplicity.

Light: 21″ ÷ 9 = 2.3″
   2.3″ × 8 = 18.4″ *(Round up to 18.5″.)*
Medium: 8.5″ ÷ 9 = .94″
   .94″ × 8 = 7.52″ *(Round up to 7.75″.)*
Dark: 26″ ÷ 9 = 2.9″
   2.9″ × 8 = 23.2″ *(Round up to 23.25″.)*

Step 3: Add in an extra strip width and 3″ for fabric straightening.

Light: 18.5″ + 3.5″ + 3″ = 25.0″
Medium: 7.75″ + 2.125″ + 3″ = 12.9″
Dark: 23.25″ + 3.25″ + 3″ = 29.5″

Step 4: Convert inches to yards, rounding up to the nearest 1/8 yard.

Light: 25.0″ rounds up to ¾ yard.
Medium: 12.9″ rounds up to ⅜ yard.
Dark: 29.5″ rounds up to ⅞ yard.

In this case, only the medium and dark yardages changed. Each dropped by ⅛ yard, which indicates that one less strip is needed for each of the fabrics. This method for determining yardage is a close estimate rather than exact. The extra strip allowed for in the calculations and the rounding up to the nearest ⅛ yard are the fudge factor. For the strip quantity to cut for a particular shape and for fewer blocks, start with fewer strips and add as needed. For more blocks, start with the number of strips listed in the table and add as needed.

For quilt designs made with two to six blocks and eleven blocks, figure the amount of fabric as described here. Once you have the yardage, there are two ways to cut the strips: Sara's method (cut one strip at a time as it is needed for the blocks) and Marci's method (cut one strip, see how many shapes can be cut from that, and then cut the rest of the strips).

The yardage just figured assumes all eight blocks use the same supporting fabrics. To make it coordinated with more depth and interest, select different fabrics for each of the different shapes. To be sure you can get the quantity needed per block from the strip(s), note how many strips have to be cut.

If a particular shape needs nine strips or less for nine blocks, then one strip per block will work. If the strip for the shape is 4″ or less, ⅛ yard for each block plus an extra ⅛ yard for a miscut is good.

If the shape requires ten or more strips for nine blocks, then two strips per block is what is needed. If the strip is 3½″, then that is 7″. So a ¼ yard will cover that shape. For larger shapes or strips, ⅜ yard or ½ yard is needed.

To make it easy, a new chart (next page) shows the yardage and cutting for an eight-block quilt. If you do your own calculations for quilts that don't have the standard nine blocks, we suggest that you make a similar chart for reference. *Please note:* The placement of the light, medium, and dark fabrics are different in our quilt than in the nine-block chart. This new chart reflects those changes.

Making the Knotted Cord Blocks

YARDAGE AND CUTTING FOR EIGHT BLOCKS

Cut the strips and corresponding shapes using the instructions on the pages noted in the table.

FABRIC	YDG FOR 8 BLOCKS	STRIP QTY AND SIZE TO CUT FOR 8 BLOCKS	QTY, SHAPE, AND SIZE TO CUT FOR 8 BLOCKS	QTY OF SHAPE IN 1 BLOCK
REPEAT (R) (A set is 6 layers.)	Minimum of 16″ repeat or 2¾ yards	3 stacked strip sets 4⅝″ × 20″	8 diamond sets 4⅝″ (page 117)	1 set of 6
LIGHT (L)	¾ yard	6 strips 3½″ × WOF	96 triangles 3½″ (page 116)	12
MEDIUM (M)	⅜ yard	3 strips 2⅛″ × WOF	96 triangles 2⅛″ (page 116)	12
DARK (D)	⅞ yard	7 strips 3¼″ × WOF	48 flat pyramids 6¼″ (page 121)	6

PIECING

Review General Information for Making Blocks (page 32). Seam allowances are ¼″ unless otherwise noted. Follow the arrows for pressing directions.

1. Determine the best selection of a 4⅝″ repeat-fabric triangle set (see Cutting the Strips, page 18). After the shapes are cut, refer to Design Possibilities (page 18) for ideas on how the shapes can be rotated for different looks. When you've determined the best look for each set of shapes, mark the center so you can piece them together appropriately. At the other end, trim off a 3″ triangle to make the gem shape.

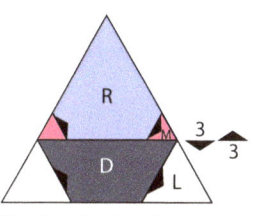
Knotted Cord wedge

2. Using 1 repeat-fabric gem shape, 2 L triangles, 2 M triangles, and 1 D flat pyramid, arrange 1 wedge.

3. Sew the 2 M triangles to the sides of the repeat-fabric gem shape to make the upper unit.

4. Sew the 2 L triangles to the D flat pyramid to make the lower unit.

5. Join the upper and lower units to complete 1 wedge.

6. Make 6 identical wedges, pressing the seam between the units up for 3 wedges and down for 3 wedges.

7. Arrange the wedges into a hexagon, with the repeat fabric at the center. Alternate the direction of the seam between the units.

8. Sew the wedges into groups of 3 to make half-hexagons. Then sew the center seam to complete the block. Refer to Sewing and Pressing Options (page 32) as needed.

Making the Chestnut Setting Triangles

With the blocks done, the setting triangles are next. The cutting and yardage calculations for setting triangles is for 24 triangles. If your quilt uses a different number of setting triangles, you'll need to do some simple calculations similar to the ones used for calculating yardage and cutting for the main blocks.

FIGURING YARDAGE FOR SETTING TRIANGLES

For the eight-block quilt in this example, you need 18 setting triangles. Using the standard table for 24 Chestnut setting triangles (page 103), figure the yardage as follows, using Conversion Chart—Fractions to Decimals (page 23) as needed.

YARDAGE AND CUTTING FOR 24 CHESTNUT SETTING TRIANGLES

FABRIC	YDG FOR 24 SETTING TRIANGLES	STRIP QTY AND SIZE TO CUT FOR 24 SETTING TRIANGLES	QTY, SHAPE, AND SIZE TO CUT FOR 24 SETTING TRIANGLES	QTY OF SHAPE IN 1 SETTING TRIANGLE
LIGHT (L)	⅝ yard	4 strips 3½″ × WOF	72 triangles 3½″ (page 116)	3
MEDIUM (M)	1 yard	8 strips 3¼″ × WOF	72 diamonds 3¼″ (page 117)	3

Light:

Step 1: Figure the number of inches needed for each fabric for 24 triangles using the chart.

Use quantity × size of strip: 4 × 3.5″ = 14″.

Step 2: Figure the amount needed for 18 blocks.

Divide the number from Step 1 by 24 to get the number of inches per block: 14″ ÷ 24 = .58″.

Then multiply by 18 for 18 blocks: .58″ × 18 = 10.44″.

Round up to nearest ¼″ for simplicity: Round up to 10.5″.

Step 3: Add in an extra strip width and 3″ for fabric straightening.

10.5″ + 3.5″ + 3″ = 17″

Step 4: Convert inches to yards, rounding up to the nearest 1/8 yard.

Use Conversion Chart—Inches to Yards (page 23) as needed.

17″ rounds up to ½ yard.

Medium:

Following the instructions in Steps 1–4 for the light fabric, do the calculations for the medium fabric.

Step 1: 8 × 3.25″ = 26″

Step 2: 26″ ÷ 24 = 1.1″
1.1″ × 18 = 19.8 *(Round up to 20″.)*

Step 3: 20″ + 3.25″ + 3″ = 26.25″

Step 4: 26.25″ rounds up to ¾ yard.

YARDAGE AND CUTTING FOR EIGHTEEN CHESTNUT SETTING TRIANGLES

Cut the strips and corresponding shapes using the instructions on the pages noted in the table.

FABRIC	YDG FOR 18 SETTING TRIANGLES	STRIP QTY AND SIZE TO CUT FOR 18 SETTING TRIANGLES	QTY, SHAPE, AND SIZE TO CUT FOR 18 SETTING TRIANGLES	QTY OF SHAPE IN 1 SETTING TRIANGLE
LIGHT (L)	½ yard	3 strips 3½″ × WOF	54 triangles 3½″ (page 116)	3
MEDIUM (M)	¾ yard	6 strips 3¼″ × WOF	54 diamonds 3¼″ (page 117)	3

Setting Triangle Cutting and Piecing

Seam allowances are ¼″ unless otherwise noted. Follow the arrows for pressing directions.

1. Using 3 M diamonds and 3 L triangles, arrange 1 setting triangle. Fig A

2. Sew 2 M diamonds to 1 L triangle. Sew 2 L triangles to 1 M diamond.

3. Join the units to complete 1 setting triangle.

4. Make 18 setting triangles. Fig B

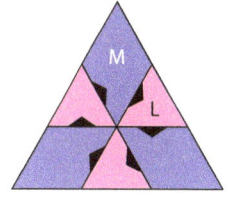

A. Chestnut setting triangle

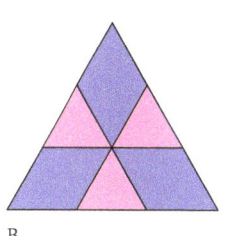

B.

Quilt Design

YARDAGE AND CUTTING FOR QUILT ASSEMBLY

FABRIC	YDG	STRIP QTY AND SIZE TO CUT	QTY AND SHAPE TO CUT
END PIECES	½ yard	2 strips 5½″ × WOF, subcut into 6 rectangles 5½ × 9½	6 L and 6 R triangle halves (page 115)
BORDER 1	⅝ yard	6 strips 2½″ × WOF	
BORDER 2	1⅜ yards	7 strips 6½″ × WOF	
BINDING	¾ yard	8 strips your favorite size	
BATTING	73″ × 80″		
BACKING	4¾ yards		

QUILT ASSEMBLY

1. Arrange the blocks, setting triangles, and end pieces into the 8-block quilt design, as shown in the quilt assembly diagram (page 86).

2. Sew each block and its corresponding triangles and end pieces to create diamond and partial diamond units.

3. Join the diamond and end units in each column.

4. Sew the columns together to complete the central part of the quilt.

5. Add borders, layer the pieced top with the batting and backing, quilt, and bind.

NOTE
Remember that we show two ways to approach these projects: Sara's way, with an artist's style, and Marci's way, with an engineer's style. Pick the way that fits your style, and above all else, have fun!

Eight-Block Quilt quilt assembly

Eight-Block Quilt 31

BLOCK DESIGNS

General Information for Making Blocks

Sewing and Pressing Options

All the quilts are made from six wedges sewn together into a hexagon. Sara and Marci each have their favorite way to piece and press the blocks.

- Sara leaves the 60° points on the shapes to use them for alignment when the wedges come together. When she joins the wedges, one wedge is sewn on and the seam is finger-pressed away from the center. Then the other wedge is added. The second seam is also finger-pressed away from the center. Both sides of the hexagon are made this way.

Important Note on Yardage

- The repeat fabric listed in each block's yardage and cutting table includes enough fabric for 9 blocks and 24 sets of 3½″ triangles to be used as setting triangles, if desired.

- If you *are not* using the repeat fabric to make setting triangles, you can make up to eleven blocks with the given yardage. If you *are* using the repeat fabric for the setting triangles and you are making more than nine blocks, you need to allow for one more strip of repeat. This will be determined by the size of the repeat shape in your chosen block. If it is 6½″, then add this to the minimum repeat. This might be 16″ + 6¼″ for a 22¼″ repeat.

- Refer to *Eight-Block Quilt* (page 27) to figure out how to reduce yardage if a different type of setting triangle is used. Or use the extra fabric in the borders, backing, or another project.

The tips of the fabric align in the middle. Pin the points of the design together and sew. Trim the tips only if they will show through a light fabric.

- Marci trims the 60° points when the shapes are initially cut using the Corner Cut 60 because she finds it faster sewing at the machine. Then she sews and presses in a direction that results in locking or nesting seams, eliminating pinning. The halves are sewn and pressed in a clockwise order (counterclockwise when viewed from the wrong side). For the right half, the top two wedges are sewn and the seam pressed down; then the third wedge is added and the seam is pressed down.

The left half starts with the bottom two wedges sewn and pressed up. Then the third wedge is joined and the seam is pressed up. When the two halves are joined, the center seam is pressed with half one way and the other half the other way, allowing all the seams to be clockwise. By sewing and pressing in this order, the bulk is reduced to a minimal amount and the seams lock in place easily. This is also known as *spinning the seams*.

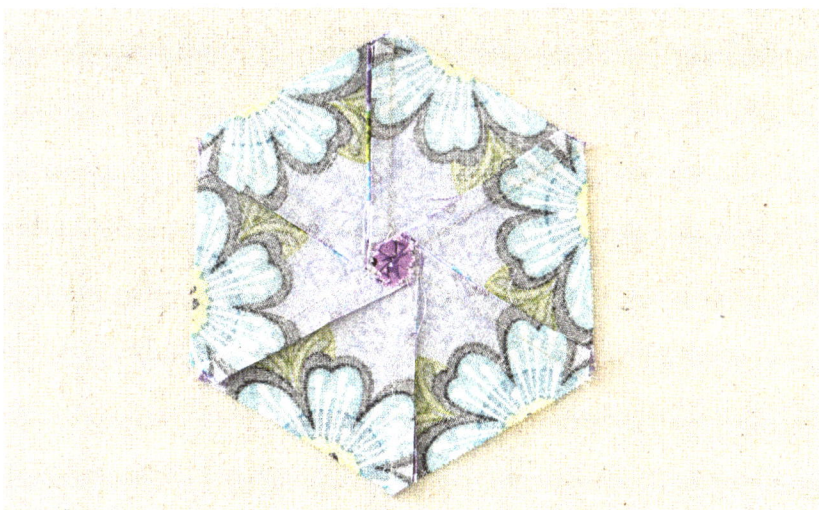

The blocks have additional pieces in each wedge, arranged into units. Make six identical wedges, pressing the seam between the units up for three wedges and down for three wedges. Arrange the wedges into a hexagon, with the repeat fabric at the center. Alternate the direction of the seam between the units.

BADGE

Finished Badge block: 16½" × 19"

The following yardage is for up to nine blocks, with all the blocks created from the same fabrics. If a variety of fabrics is desired throughout the nine blocks, read Using Multiple Fabrics per Shape (page 23) to figure yardage. Refer to General Information for Making Blocks (page 32) as needed.

YARDAGE AND CUTTING

Cut the strips and corresponding shapes using the instructions on the pages noted in the table. Refer to Cutting the Strips (page 18) as needed.

FABRIC	YDG FOR 9 BLOCKS	STRIP QTY AND SIZE TO CUT FOR 9 BLOCKS	QTY, SHAPE, AND SIZE TO CUT FOR 9 BLOCKS	QTY OF SHAPE IN 1 BLOCK
REPEAT (R) (A set is 6 layers.)	Minimum of 24" repeat or 4 yards	3 stacked strip sets 6¼" × 20"	9 triangle sets 6¼" (page 116)	1 set of 6
LIGHT (L)	½ yard	3 strips 3½" × WOF	54 triangles 3½" (page 116)	6
MEDIUM (M)	1¼ yards	11 strips 3¼" × WOF	108 flat pyramids 4⅞" (page 121)	12

Piecing

Review General Information for Making Blocks (page 32). Seam allowances are ¼" unless otherwise noted. Follow the arrows for pressing directions.

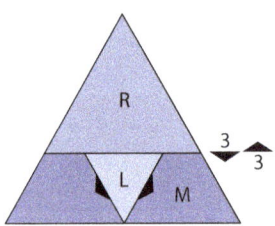

Badge wedge

1. Determine the best selection of a 6¼" R triangle set (see Cutting the Strips, page 18). After the shapes are cut, refer to Design Possibilities (page 18) for ideas on how the shapes can be rotated for different looks. When you've determined the best look for each set of shapes, mark the center so you can piece them together appropriately.

2. Using 1 R triangle, 1 L triangle, and 2 M flat pyramids, arrange 1 wedge.

3. Sew the 2 M flat pyramids on either side of the L triangle. Attach the R triangle to complete 1 wedge.

4. Make 6 identical wedges.

5. Arrange the wedges into a hexagon, with the repeat fabric at the center.

6. Sew the wedges into groups of 3 to make half-hexagons. Then sew the center seam to complete the block. Refer to Sewing and Pressing Options (page 32) as needed.

BEZEL

Finished Bezel block: 16½˝ × 19˝

The following yardage is for up to nine blocks, with all the blocks created from the same fabrics. If a variety of fabrics is desired throughout the nine blocks, read Using Multiple Fabrics per Shape (page 23) to figure yardage. Refer to General Information for Making Blocks (page 32) as needed.

YARDAGE AND CUTTING

Cut the strips and corresponding shapes using the instructions on the pages noted in the table. Refer to Cutting the Strips (page 18) as needed.

FABRIC	YDG FOR 9 BLOCKS	STRIP QTY AND SIZE TO CUT FOR 9 BLOCKS	QTY, SHAPE, AND SIZE TO CUT FOR 9 BLOCKS	QTY OF SHAPE IN 1 BLOCK
REPEAT (R) (A set is 6 layers.)	Minimum of 18˝ repeat or 3 yards	2 stacked strip sets 5˝ × 20˝	9 triangle sets 5˝ (page 116)	1 set of 6
LIGHT (L)	⅞ yard	6 strips 3½˝ × WOF	108 triangles 3½˝ (page 116)	12
MEDIUM (M)	⅝ yard	9 strips 1¾˝ × WOF	54 flat pyramids 6¼˝ (page 121)	6
DARK (D)	1 yard	8 strips 3¼˝ × WOF	54 flat pyramids 6¼˝ (page 121)	6

Piecing

Review General Information for Making Blocks (page 32). Seam allowances are ¼˝ unless otherwise noted. Follow the arrows for pressing directions.

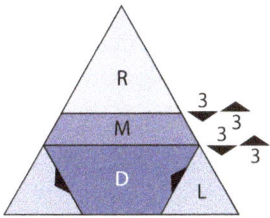

Bezel wedge

1. Determine the best selection of a 5˝ R triangle set (see Cutting the Strips, page 18). After the shapes are cut, refer to Design Possibilities (page 18) for ideas on how the shapes can be rotated for different looks. When you've determined the best look for each set of shapes, mark the center so you can piece them together appropriately.

2. Using 1 R triangle, 2 L triangles, 1 M flat pyramid, and 1 D flat pyramid, arrange 1 wedge.

3. Attach the R triangle to the M flat pyramid to make the upper unit.

4. Sew the 2 L triangles to either side of the D flat pyramid to make the lower unit.

5. Join the upper and lower units to complete 1 wedge.

6. Make 6 identical wedges.

7. Arrange the wedges into a hexagon, with the repeat fabric at the center.

8. Sew the wedges into groups of 3 to make half-hexagons. Then sew the center seam to complete the block. Refer to Sewing and Pressing Options (page 32) as needed.

BOLD STAR

Finished Bold Star block: 16½″ × 19″

The following yardage is for up to nine blocks, with all the blocks created from the same fabrics. If a variety of fabrics is desired throughout the nine blocks, read Using Multiple Fabrics per Shape (page 23) to figure yardage. Refer to General Information for Making Blocks (page 32) as needed.

YARDAGE AND CUTTING

Cut the strips and corresponding shapes using the instructions on the pages noted in the table. Refer to Cutting the Strips (page 18) as needed.

FABRIC	YDG FOR 9 BLOCKS	STRIP QTY AND SIZE TO CUT FOR 9 BLOCKS	QTY, SHAPE, AND SIZE TO CUT FOR 9 BLOCKS	QTY OF SHAPE IN 1 BLOCK
REPEAT (R) (A set is 6 layers.)	Minimum of 18″ repeat or 3 yards	3 stacked strip sets 3¼″ × 20″	9 diamond sets 3¼″ (page 117)	1 set of 6
LIGHT (L)	⅞ yard	12 strips 2⅛″ × WOF	108 half-diamonds 2⅛″ (page 122)	12
DARK (D)	⅞ yard	12 strips 2⅛″ × WOF		
MEDIUM 1 (M1)	½ yard	3 strips 3½″ × WOF	54 triangles 3½″ (page 116)	6
MEDIUM 2 (M2)	⅞ yard	6 strips 3½″ × WOF	108 triangles 3½″ (page 116)	12

Piecing

Review General Information for Making Blocks (page 32). Seam allowances are ¼″ unless otherwise noted. Follow the arrows for pressing directions.

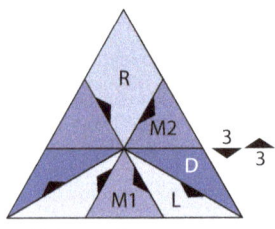

Bold Star wedge

1. Determine the best selection of a 3¼″ R diamond set (see Cutting the Strips, page 18). After the shapes are cut, refer to Design Possibilities (page 18) for ideas on how the shapes can be rotated for different looks. When you've determined the best look for each set of shapes, mark the center so you can piece them together appropriately.

2. Using 1 R diamond, 2 L-D matched half-diamonds, 1 M1 triangle, and 2 M2 triangles, arrange 1 wedge.

3. Sew the 2 L-D matched half-diamonds to either side of the M1 triangle, with the light fabric toward the triangle, to make the lower unit.

4. Sew the 2 M2 triangles to the non-center edges of the R diamond to make the upper unit.

5. Join the upper and lower units to complete 1 wedge.

6. Make 6 identical wedges.

7. Arrange the wedges into a hexagon, with the repeat fabric at the center.

8. Sew the wedges into groups of 3 to make half-hexagons. Then sew the center seam to complete the block. Refer to Sewing and Pressing Options (page 32) as needed.

BUTTON

Finished Button block: 16½″ × 19″

The following yardage is for up to nine blocks, with all the blocks created from the same fabrics. If a variety of fabrics is desired throughout the nine blocks, read Using Multiple Fabrics per Shape (page 23) to figure yardage. Refer to General Information for Making Blocks (page 32) as needed.

YARDAGE AND CUTTING

Cut the strips and corresponding shapes using the instructions on the pages noted in the table. Refer to Cutting the Strips (page 18) as needed.

FABRIC	YDG FOR 9 BLOCKS	STRIP QTY AND SIZE TO CUT FOR 9 BLOCKS	QTY, SHAPE, AND SIZE TO CUT FOR 9 BLOCKS	QTY OF SHAPE IN 1 BLOCK
REPEAT (R) (A set is 6 layers.)	Minimum of 20″ repeat or 3⅝ yards	2 stacked strip sets 4⅝″ × 20″	9 diamond sets 4⅝″ (page 117)	1 set of 6
LIGHT (L)	½ yard	4 strips 2⅛″ × WOF	108 triangles 2⅛″ (page 116)	12
MEDIUM (M)	½ yard	3 strips 3½″ × WOF	54 triangles 3½″ (page 116)	6
DARK (D)	1¼ yards	11 strips 3¼″ × WOF	108 diamonds 3¼″ (page 117)	12

Piecing

Review General Information for Making Blocks (page 32). Seam allowances are ¼″ unless otherwise noted. Follow the arrows for pressing directions.

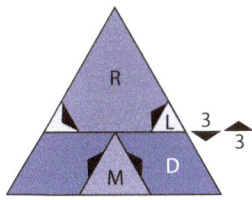

Button wedge

1. Determine the best selection of a 4⅝″ R diamond set (see Cutting the Strips, page 18). After the shapes are cut, refer to Design Possibilities (page 18) for ideas on how the shapes can be rotated for different looks. When you've determined the best look for each set of shapes, mark the center so you can piece them together appropriately. On the other end, trim off a 3″ triangle to make the gem shape (page 121).

2. Using 1 R gem shape, 2 L triangles, 1 M triangle, and 2 D diamonds, arrange 1 wedge.

3. Sew the 2 L triangles to the sides of the R gem shape to make the upper unit.

4. Sew the 2 D diamonds on either side of the M triangle to make the lower unit.

5. Join the upper and lower units to complete 1 wedge.

6. Make 6 identical wedges.

7. Arrange the wedges into a hexagon, with the repeat fabric at the center.

8. Sew the wedges into groups of 3 to make half-hexagons. Then sew the center seam to complete the block. Refer to Sewing and Pressing Options (page 32) as needed.

Block Designs

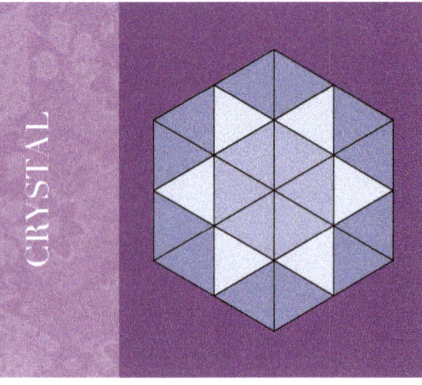

CRYSTAL

Finished Crystal block: 11″ × 12½″

The following yardage is for up to nine blocks, with all the blocks created from the same fabrics. If a variety of fabrics is desired throughout the nine blocks, read Using Multiple Fabrics per Shape (page 23) to figure yardage. Refer to General Information for Making Blocks (page 32) as needed. This block is smaller than most and requires a setting triangle cut at 6¼″.

YARDAGE AND CUTTING

Cut the strips and corresponding shapes using the instructions on the pages noted in the table. Refer to Cutting the Strips (page 18) as needed.

FABRIC	YDG FOR 9 BLOCKS	STRIP QTY AND SIZE TO CUT FOR 9 BLOCKS	QTY, SHAPE, AND SIZE TO CUT FOR 9 BLOCKS	QTY OF SHAPE IN 1 BLOCK
REPEAT (R) (A set is 6 layers.)	Minimum of 18″ repeat or 3 yards	2 stacked strip sets 3½″ × 20″	9 triangle sets 3½″ (page 116)	1 set of 6
LIGHT (L)	½ yard	3 strips 3½″ × WOF	54 triangles 3½″ (page 116)	6
MEDIUM (M)	⅞ yard	6 strips 3½″ × WOF	108 triangles 3½″ (page 116)	12

Piecing

Review General Information for Making Blocks (page 32). Seam allowances are ¼″ unless otherwise noted. Follow the arrows for pressing directions.

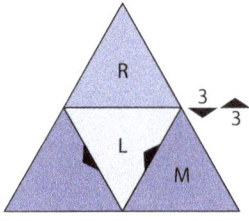

Crystal wedge

1. Determine the best selection of a 3½″ R triangle set (see Cutting the Strips, page 18). After the shapes are cut, refer to Design Possibilities (page 18) for ideas on how the shapes can be rotated for different looks. When you've determined the best look for each set of shapes, mark the center so you can piece them together appropriately.

2. Using 1 R triangle, 1 L triangle, and 2 M triangles, arrange 1 wedge.

3. Sew the 2 M triangles to the sides of the L triangle. Attach the R triangle.

4. Make 6 identical wedges.

5. Arrange the wedges into a hexagon, with the repeat fabric at the center.

6. Sew the wedges into groups of 3 to make half-hexagons. Then sew the center seam to complete the block. Refer to Sewing and Pressing Options (page 32) as needed.

DAINTY

Finished Dainty block: 16½″ × 19″

The following yardage is for up to nine blocks, with all the blocks created from the same fabrics. If a variety of fabrics is desired throughout the nine blocks, read Using Multiple Fabrics per Shape (page 23) to figure yardage. Refer to General Information for Making Blocks (page 32) as needed.

YARDAGE AND CUTTING

Cut the strips and corresponding shapes using the instructions on the pages noted in the table. Refer to Cutting the Strips (page 18) as needed.

FABRIC	YDG FOR 9 BLOCKS	STRIP QTY AND SIZE TO CUT FOR 9 BLOCKS	QTY, SHAPE, AND SIZE TO CUT FOR 9 BLOCKS	QTY OF SHAPE IN 1 BLOCK
REPEAT (R) (A set is 6 layers.)	Minimum of 20″ repeat or 3½ yards	3 stacked strip sets 4⅝″ × 20″	9 diamond sets 4⅝″ (page 117)	1 set of 6
LIGHT 1 (L1)	½ yard	4 strips 2⅛″ × WOF	108 triangles 2⅛″ (page 116)	12
LIGHT 2 (L2)	½ yard	3 strips 3½″ × WOF	54 triangles 3½″ (page 116)	6
MEDIUM (M)	1¼ yards	11 strips 3¼″ × WOF	108 flat pyramids 4⅞″ (page 121)	12

Piecing

Review General Information for Making Blocks (page 32). Seam allowances are ¼″ unless otherwise noted. Follow the arrows for pressing directions.

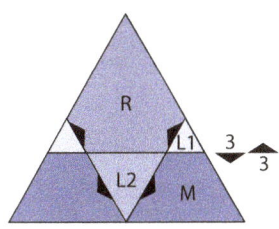

Dainty wedge

1. Determine the best selection of a 4⅝″ R diamond set (see Cutting the Strips, page 18). After the shapes are cut, refer to Design Possibilities (page 18) for ideas on how the shapes can be rotated for different looks. When you've determined the best look for each set of shapes, mark the center so you can piece them together appropriately. At the other end, trim off a 3″ triangle to make the gem shape (page 121).

2. Using 1 R gem shape, 2 L1 triangles, 1 L2 triangle, and 2 M flat pyramids, arrange 1 wedge.

3. Sew the 2 L1 triangles to the sides of the R gem shape to make the upper unit.

4. Sew the 2 M flat pyramids to either side of the L2 triangle to make the lower unit.

5. Join the upper and lower units to finish 1 wedge.

6. Make 6 identical wedges.

7. Arrange the wedges into a hexagon, with the repeat fabric at the center.

8. Sew the wedges into groups of 3 to make half-hexagons. Then sew the center seam to complete the block. Refer to Sewing and Pressing Options (page 32) as needed.

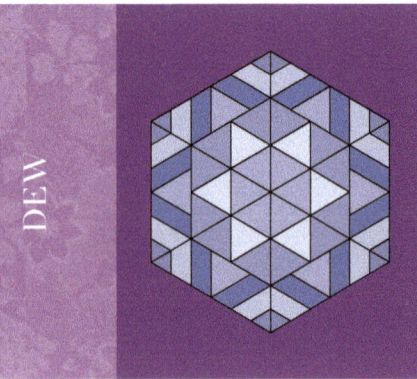

DEW

Finished Dew block: 16½″ × 19″

The following yardage is for up to nine blocks, with all the blocks created from the same fabrics. If a variety of fabrics is desired throughout the nine blocks, read Using Multiple Fabrics per Shape (page 23) to figure yardage. Refer to General Information for Making Blocks (page 32) as needed.

YARDAGE AND CUTTING

Cut the strips and corresponding shapes using the instructions on the pages noted in the table. Refer to Cutting the Strips (page 18) as needed.

FABRIC	YDG FOR 9 BLOCKS	STRIP QTY AND SIZE TO CUT FOR 9 BLOCKS	QTY, SHAPE, AND SIZE TO CUT FOR 9 BLOCKS	QTY OF SHAPE IN 1 BLOCK
REPEAT (R) (A set is 6 layers.)	Minimum of 18″ repeat or 3 yards	2 stacked strip sets 3½″ × 20″	9 triangle sets 3½″ (page 116)	1 set of 6
LIGHT 1 (L1)	½ yard	3 strips 3½″ × WOF	54 triangles 3½″ (page 116)	6
MEDIUM 1 (M1)	⅞ yard	6 strips 3½″ × WOF	108 triangles 3½″ (page 116)	12
MEDIUM 2 (M2)	½ yard	3 strips 3½″ × WOF	54 triangles 3½″ (page 116)	6
LIGHT 2 (L2)	⅞ yard	12 strips 1⅞″ × WOF	108 strip-pieced triangles 3½″ (page 116)	12
MEDIUM 3 (M3)	½ yard	6 strips 2⅛″ × WOF		
DARK (D)	¾ yard	11 strips 1⅞″ × WOF	108 long diamonds 3¼″ (54 L and 54 R) (page 118)	12 (6 L and 6 R)

Piecing

Review General Information for Making Blocks (page 32). Seam allowances are ¼″ unless otherwise noted. Follow the arrows for pressing directions.

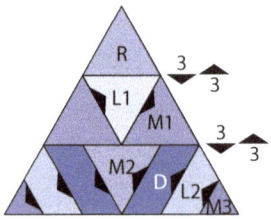

Dew wedge

1. Determine the best selection of a 3½″ R triangle set (see Cutting the Strips, page 18). After the shapes are cut, refer to Design Possibilities (page 18) for ideas on how the shapes can be rotated for different looks. Mark the center so you can piece them together appropriately.

2. Using 1 R triangle, 1 L1 triangle, 2 M1 triangles, 1 M2 triangle, 2 D long diamonds (1 left and 1 right), and 2 L2-M3 strip-pieced triangles, arrange 1 wedge.

3. Sew the 2 M1 triangles to 2 sides of the L1 triangle. Attach the R triangle to make the upper unit.

4. Sew the 2D long diamonds to 2 sides of the M2 triangle. Add 2 L2-M3 strip-pieced triangles to make the lower unit.

5. Join the upper and lower units to make 1 wedge.

6. Make 6 identical wedges.

7. Arrange the wedges into a hexagon, with the repeat fabric at the center.

8. Sew the wedges into groups of 3 to make half-hexagons. Then sew the center seam to complete the block. Refer to Sewing and Pressing Options (page 32) as needed.

DUTCH STAR

Finished Dutch Star block: 16½″ × 19″

The following yardage is for up to nine blocks, with all the blocks created from the same fabrics. If a variety of fabrics is desired throughout the nine blocks, read Using Multiple Fabrics per Shape (page 23) to figure yardage. Refer to General Information for Making Blocks (page 32) as needed.

YARDAGE AND CUTTING

Cut the strips and corresponding shapes using the instructions on the pages noted in the table. Refer to Cutting the Strips (page 18) as needed.

FABRIC	YDG FOR 9 BLOCKS	STRIP QTY AND SIZE TO CUT FOR 9 BLOCKS	QTY, SHAPE, AND SIZE TO CUT FOR 9 BLOCKS	QTY OF SHAPE IN 1 BLOCK
REPEAT (R) (A set is 6 layers.)	Minimum of 24″ repeat or 4 yards	3 stacked strip sets 6¼″ × 20″	9 triangle sets 6¼″ (page 116)	1 set of 6
LIGHT (L)	⅞ yard	12 strips 2⅛″ × WOF	108 half-diamonds 2⅛″ (page 122)	12
DARK (D)	⅞ yard	12 strips 2⅛″ × WOF		
MEDIUM (M)	½ yard	3 strips 3½″ × WOF	54 triangles 3½″ (page 116)	6

Piecing

Review General Information for Making Blocks (page 32). Seam allowances are ¼″ unless otherwise noted. Follow the arrows for pressing directions.

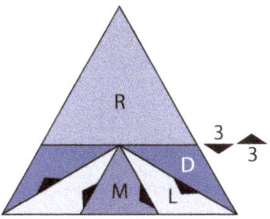

Dutch Star wedge

1. Determine the best selection of a 6¼″ R triangle set (see Cutting the Strips, page 18). After the shapes are cut, refer to Design Possibilities (page 18) for ideas on how the shapes can be rotated for different looks. When you've determined the best look for each set of shapes, mark the center so you can piece them together appropriately.

2. Using 1 R triangle, 2 L-D matched half-diamonds, and 1 M triangle, arrange 1 wedge.

3. Sew the 2 L-D matched half-diamonds to either side of the M triangle, with the light fabric next to the triangle. Attach the R triangle.

4. Make 6 identical wedges.

5. Arrange the wedges into a hexagon, with the repeat fabric at the center.

6. Sew the wedges into groups of 3 to make half-hexagons. Then sew the center seam to complete the block. Refer to Sewing and Pressing Options (page 32) as needed.

Block Designs 41

FLASHDANCE

Finished Flashdance block: 16½″ × 19″

The following yardage is for up to nine blocks, with all the blocks created from the same fabrics. If a variety of fabrics is desired throughout the nine blocks, read Using Multiple Fabrics per Shape (page 23) to figure yardage. Refer to General Information for Making Blocks (page 32) as needed.

YARDAGE AND CUTTING

Cut the strips and corresponding shapes using the instructions on the pages noted in the table. Refer to Cutting the Strips (page 18) as needed.

FABRIC	YDG FOR 9 BLOCKS	STRIP QTY AND SIZE TO CUT FOR 9 BLOCKS	QTY, SHAPE, AND SIZE TO CUT FOR 9 BLOCKS	QTY OF SHAPE IN 1 BLOCK
REPEAT (R) (A set is 6 layers.)	Minimum of 18″ repeat or 3 yards	3 stacked strip sets 3¼″ × 20″	9 diamond sets 3¼″ (page 117)	1 set of 6
LIGHT 1 (L1)	⅞ yard	6 strips 3½″ × WOF	108 triangles 3½″ (page 116)	12
LIGHT 2 (L2)	⅝ yard	7 strips 2⅛″ × WOF	216 matched triangles 2⅛″ (page 122)	24
DARK (D)	⅝ yard	7 strips 2⅛″ × WOF		
MEDIUM 1 (M1)	½ yard	3 strips 3½″ × WOF	54 triangles 3½″ (page 116)	6
MEDIUM 2 (M2)	⅞ yard	6 strips 3½″ × WOF	108 triangles 3½″ (page 116)	12

Piecing

Review General Information for Making Blocks (page 32). Seam allowances are ¼″ unless otherwise noted. Follow the arrows for pressing directions.

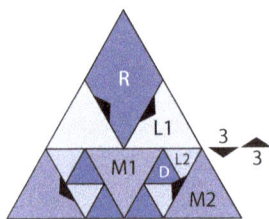

Flashdance wedge

1. Determine the best selection of a 3¼″ R diamond set (see Cutting the Strips, page 18). After the shapes are cut, refer to Design Possibilities (page 18) for ideas on how the shapes can be rotated for different looks. Mark the center so you can piece them together appropriately.

2. Using 1 R diamond, 4 L2-D matched triangles, 2 L1 triangles, 1 M1 triangle, and 2 M2 triangles, arrange 1 wedge.

3. Sew the 2 L1 triangles to the non-center edges of the diamond to make the upper unit.

4. Sew the 4 L2-D matched triangles into 2 pairs so that they are a mirror image, as shown.

5. Sew these pieced triangle units to either side of the M1 triangle. Add 2 M2 triangles on either end to make the lower unit.

6. Join the upper and lower units to complete 1 wedge.

7. Make 6 identical wedges.

8. Arrange the wedges into a hexagon, with the repeat fabric at the center.

9. Sew the wedges into groups of 3 to make half-hexagons. Then sew the center seam to complete the block. Refer to Sewing and Pressing Options (page 32) as needed.

FLINT

Finished Flint block: 16½″ × 19″

The following yardage is for up to nine blocks, with all the blocks created from the same fabrics. If a variety of fabrics is desired throughout the nine blocks, read Using Multiple Fabrics per Shape (page 23) to figure yardage. Refer to General Information for Making Blocks (page 32) as needed.

YARDAGE AND CUTTING

Cut the strips and corresponding shapes using the instructions on the pages noted in the table. Refer to Cutting the Strips (page 18) as needed.

FABRIC	YDG FOR 9 BLOCKS	STRIP QTY AND SIZE TO CUT FOR 9 BLOCKS	QTY, SHAPE, AND SIZE TO CUT FOR 9 BLOCKS	QTY OF SHAPE IN 1 BLOCK
REPEAT (R) (A set is 6 layers.)	Minimum of 18″ repeat or 3 yards	3 stacked strip sets 3¼″ × 20″	9 diamond sets 3¼″ (page 117)	1 set of 6
LIGHT (L)	½ yard	7 strips 1⅞″ × WOF	108 strip-pieced diamonds 1⅞″ (54 L and 54 R) (page 120)	12 (6 L and 6 R)
DARK (D)	½ yard	7 strips 1⅞″ × WOF		
MEDIUM 1 (M1)	½ yard	3 strips 3½″ × WOF	54 triangles 3½″ (page 116)	6
MEDIUM 2 (M2)	1¼ yards	11 strips 3¼″ × WOF	108 flat pyramids 4⅞″ (page 121)	12

Piecing

Review General Information for Making Blocks (page 32). Seam allowances are ¼″ unless otherwise noted. Follow the arrows for pressing directions.

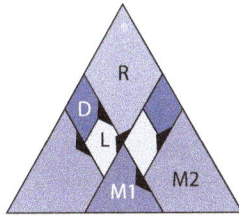

Flint wedge

1. Determine the best selection of a 3¼″ R diamond set (see Cutting the Strips, page 18). After the shapes are cut, refer to Design Possibilities (page 18) for ideas on how the shapes can be rotated for different looks. When you've determined the best look for each set of shapes, mark the center so you can piece them together appropriately.

2. Using 1 R diamond, 2 L-D strip-pieced diamonds, 1 M1 triangle, and 2 M2 flat pyramids, arrange 1 wedge.

3. Sew the 2 M2 flat pyramids to the L-D strip-pieced diamonds so they are a mirror image, as shown.

4. Attach the R diamond to the unit on the left. Sew the M1 triangle to the unit on the right.

5. Join these 2 units to complete 1 wedge.

6. Make 6 identical wedges.

7. Arrange the wedges into a hexagon, with the repeat fabric at the center.

8. Sew the wedges into groups of 3 to make half-hexagons. Then sew the center seam to complete the block. Refer to Sewing and Pressing Options (page 32) as needed.

Block Designs

FROZEN

Finished Frozen block: 16½″ × 19″

The following yardage is for up to nine blocks, with all the blocks created from the same fabrics. If a variety of fabrics is desired throughout the nine blocks, read Using Multiple Fabrics per Shape (page 23) to figure yardage. Refer to General Information for Making Blocks (page 32) as needed.

YARDAGE AND CUTTING

Cut the strips and corresponding shapes using the instructions on the pages noted in the table. Refer to Cutting the Strips (page 18) as needed.

FABRIC	YDG FOR 9 BLOCKS	STRIP QTY AND SIZE TO CUT FOR 9 BLOCKS	QTY, SHAPE, AND SIZE TO CUT FOR 9 BLOCKS	QTY OF SHAPE IN 1 BLOCK
REPEAT (R) (A set is 6 layers.)	Minimum of 24″ repeat or 4 yards	3 stacked strip sets 6¼″ × 20″	9 triangle sets 6¼″ (page 116)	1 set of 6
LIGHT (L)	½ yard	3 strips 3½″ × WOF	54 triangles 3½″ (page 116)	6
MEDIUM (M)	¾ yard	6 strips 3½″ × WOF	108 triangles 3½″ (page 116)	12
DARK (D)	¾ yard	11 strips 1⅞″ × WOF	108 long diamonds 3¼″ (54 L and 54 R) (page 118)	12 (6 L and 6 R)

Piecing

Review General Information for Making Blocks (page 32). Seam allowances are ¼″ unless otherwise noted. Follow the arrows for pressing directions.

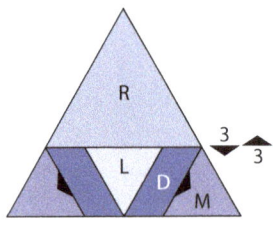

Frozen wedge

1. Determine the best selection of a 6¼″ R triangle set (see Cutting the Strips, page 18). After the shapes are cut, refer to Design Possibilities (page 18) for ideas on how the shapes can be rotated for different looks. When you've determined the best look for each set of shapes, mark the center so you can piece them together appropriately.

2. Using 1 R triangle, 1 L triangle, 2 M triangles, and 2 D long diamonds (1 left and 1 right), arrange 1 wedge.

3. Sew the D long diamonds to the M triangles so they are a mirror image, as shown. Sew to the L triangle. Attach the R triangle to complete the wedge.

4. Make 6 identical wedges.

5. Arrange the wedges into a hexagon, with the repeat fabric at the center.

6. Sew the wedges into groups of 3 to make half-hexagons. Then sew the center seam to complete the block. Refer to Sewing and Pressing Options (page 32) as needed.

KNOTTED CORD

Finished Knotted Cord block: 16½″ × 19″

The following yardage is for up to nine blocks, with all the blocks created from the same fabrics. If a variety of fabrics is desired throughout the nine blocks, read Using Multiple Fabrics per Shape (page 23) to figure yardage. Refer to General Information for Making Blocks (page 32) as needed.

YARDAGE AND CUTTING

Cut the strips and corresponding shapes using the instructions on the pages noted in the table. Refer to Cutting the Strips (page 18) as needed.

FABRIC	YDG FOR 9 BLOCKS	STRIP QTY AND SIZE TO CUT FOR 9 BLOCKS	QTY, SHAPE, AND SIZE TO CUT FOR 9 BLOCKS	QTY OF SHAPE IN 1 BLOCK
REPEAT (R) (A set is 6 layers.)	Minimum of 20″ repeat or 3½ yards	3 stacked strip sets 4⅝″ × 20″	9 diamond sets 4⅝″ (page 117)	1 set of 6
LIGHT (L)	½ yard	4 strips 2⅛″ × WOF	108 triangles 2⅛″ (page 116)	12
MEDIUM (M)	1 yard	8 strips 3¼″ × WOF	54 flat pyramids 6¼″ (page 121)	6
DARK (D)	¾ yard	6 strips 3½″ × WOF	108 triangles 3½″ (page 116)	12

Piecing

Review General Information for Making Blocks (page 32). Seam allowances are ¼″ unless otherwise noted. Follow the arrows for pressing directions.

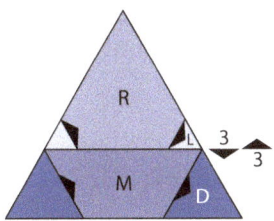

Knotted Cord wedge

1. Determine the best selection of a 4⅝″ R diamond set (see Cutting the Strips, page 18). After the shapes are cut, refer to Design Possibilities (page 18) for ideas on how the shapes can be rotated for different looks. When you've determined the best look for each set of shapes, mark the center so you can piece them together appropriately. At the other end, trim off a 3″ triangle to make the gem shape (page 121).

2. Using 1 R gem shape, 2 L triangles, 1 M flat pyramid, and 2 D triangles, arrange 1 wedge.

3. Sew the 2 L triangles to the sides of the R gem shape to make the upper unit.

4. Sew the 2 D triangles to the M flat pyramid to make the lower unit.

5. Join the upper and lower units to complete 1 wedge.

6. Make 6 identical wedges.

7. Arrange the wedges into a hexagon, with the repeat fabric at the center.

8. Sew the wedges into groups of 3 to make half-hexagons. Then sew the center seam to complete the block. Refer to Sewing and Pressing Options (page 32) as needed.

Block Designs 45

LAMP

Finished Lamp block: 11" × 12¾"

Notice that this block is smaller, so the yardage is for ten blocks instead of nine. The smaller blocks are great for making a smaller quilt. Because of the smaller block size, you will not be able to use the standard setting triangles. Either design your quilt without setting triangles (see Blocks-Only Settings, page 98) or make setting triangles using a 6¼" cut triangle.

If a variety of fabrics is desired throughout the blocks, read Using Multiple Fabrics per Shape (page 23) to figure yardage. Refer to General Information for Making Blocks (page 32) as needed. For a three-dimensional look, see *Lamp Variation* (page 100).

YARDAGE AND CUTTING

Cut the strips and corresponding shapes using the instructions on the pages noted in the table. Refer to Cutting the Strips (page 18) as needed.

FABRIC	YDG FOR 10 BLOCKS	STRIP QTY AND SIZE TO CUT FOR 10 BLOCKS	QTY, SHAPE, AND SIZE TO CUT FOR 10 BLOCKS	QTY OF SHAPE IN 1 BLOCK
REPEAT (R) (A set is 6 layers.)	Minimum of 9" repeat or 1½ yards	2 stacked strip sets 3½" × 20"	10 triangle sets 3½" (page 116)	1 set of 6
LIGHT (L)	1 yard	9 strips 3¼" × WOF	60 flat pyramids 6¼" (page 121)	6

Piecing

Review General Information for Making Blocks (page 32). Seam allowances are ¼" unless otherwise noted. Follow the arrows for pressing directions.

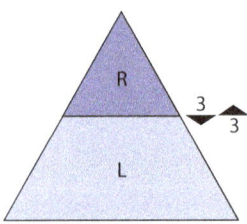

Lamp wedge

1. Determine the best selection of a 3½" R triangle set (see Cutting the Strips, page 18). After the shapes are cut, refer to Design Possibilities (page 18) for ideas on how the shapes can be rotated for different looks. When you've determined the best look for each set of shapes, mark the center so you can piece them together appropriately.

2. Using 1 R triangle and 1 L flat pyramid, arrange 1 wedge.

3. Attach the R triangle to the L flat pyramid to complete 1 wedge.

4. Make 6 identical wedges.

5. Arrange the wedges into a hexagon, with the repeat fabric at the center.

6. Sew the wedges into groups of 3 to make half-hexagons. Then sew the center seam to complete the block. Refer to Sewing and Pressing Options (page 32) as needed.

LITTLE GARDEN

Finished Little Garden block: 16½˝ × 19˝

The following yardage is for up to nine blocks, with all the blocks created from the same fabrics. If a variety of fabrics is desired throughout the nine blocks, read Using Multiple Fabrics per Shape (page 23) to figure yardage. Refer to General Information for Making Blocks (page 32) as needed.

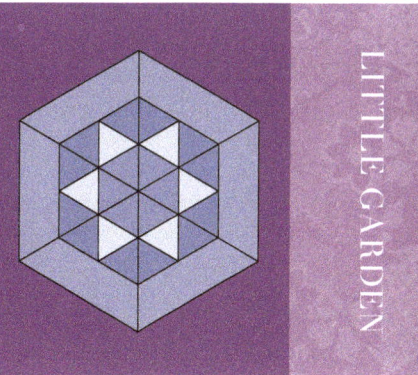

YARDAGE AND CUTTING

Cut the strips and corresponding shapes using the instructions on the pages noted in the table. Refer to Cutting the Strips (page 18) as needed.

FABRIC	YDG FOR 9 BLOCKS	STRIP QTY AND SIZE TO CUT FOR 9 BLOCKS	QTY, SHAPE, AND SIZE TO CUT FOR 9 BLOCKS	QTY OF SHAPE IN 1 BLOCK
REPEAT (R) (A set is 6 layers.)	Minimum of 18˝ repeat or 3 yards	2 stacked strip sets 3½˝ × 20˝	9 triangle sets 3½˝ (page 116)	1 set of 6
LIGHT (L)	½ yard	3 strips 3½˝ × WOF	54 triangles 3½˝ (page 116)	6
MEDIUM (M)	1½ yards	14 strips 3¼˝ × WOF	54 flat pyramids 9˝ (page 121)	6
DARK (D)	¾ yard	6 strips 3½˝ × WOF	108 triangles 3½˝ (page 116)	12

Piecing

Review General Information for Making Blocks (page 32). Seam allowances are ¼˝ unless otherwise noted. Follow the arrows for pressing directions.

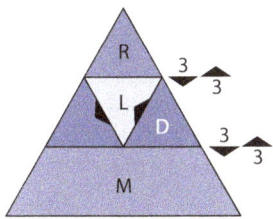

Little Garden wedge

1. Determine the best selection of a 3½˝ R triangle set (see Cutting the Strips, page 18). After the shapes are cut, refer to Design Possibilities (page 18) for ideas on how the shapes can be rotated for different looks. When you've determined the best look for each set of shapes, mark the center so you can piece them together appropriately.

2. Using 1 R triangle, 1 L triangle, 2 D triangles, and 1 M flat pyramid, arrange 1 wedge.

3. Sew the 2 D triangles to the L triangle. Add the M flat pyramid. Attach the R triangle to complete 1 wedge.

4. Make 6 identical wedges.

5. Arrange the wedges into a hexagon, with the repeat fabric at the center.

6. Sew the wedges into groups of 3 to make half-hexagons. Then sew the center seam to complete the block. Refer to Sewing and Pressing Options (page 32) as needed.

Block Designs 47

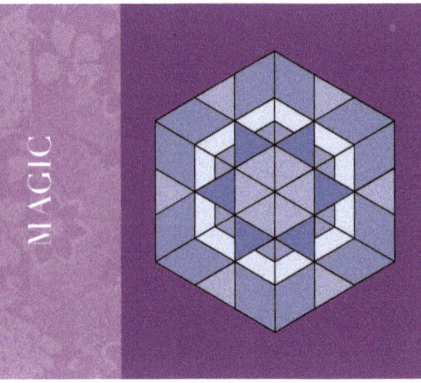

MAGIC

Finished Magic block: 16½″ × 19″

The following yardage is for up to nine blocks, with all the blocks created from the same fabrics. If a variety of fabrics is desired throughout the nine blocks, read Using Multiple Fabrics per Shape (page 23) to figure yardage. Refer to General Information for Making Blocks (page 32) as needed.

YARDAGE AND CUTTING

Cut the strips and corresponding shapes using the instructions on the pages noted in the table. Refer to Cutting the Strips (page 18) as needed.

FABRIC	YDG FOR 9 BLOCKS	STRIP QTY AND SIZE TO CUT FOR 9 BLOCKS	QTY, SHAPE, AND SIZE TO CUT FOR 9 BLOCKS	QTY OF SHAPE IN 1 BLOCK
REPEAT (R) (A set is 6 layers.)	Minimum of 18″ repeat or 3 yards	2 stacked strip sets 3½″ × 20″	9 triangle sets 3½″ (page 116)	1 set of 6
LIGHT 1 (L1)	½ yard	3 strips 3½″ × WOF	54 triangles 3½″ (page 116)	6
MEDIUM 1 (M1)	1¼ yards	11 strips 3¼″ × WOF	108 diamonds 3¼″ (page 117)	12
LIGHT 2 (L2)	⅞ yard	12 strips 1⅞″ × WOF	108 strip-pieced triangles 3½″ (page 116)	12
MEDIUM 2 (M2)	½ yard	6 strips 2⅛″ × WOF	108 strip-pieced triangles 3½″ (page 116)	12
DARK (D)	½ yard	3 strips 3½″ × WOF	54 triangles 3½″ (page 116)	6

Piecing

Review General Information for Making Blocks (page 32). Seam allowances are ¼″ unless otherwise noted. Follow the arrows for pressing directions.

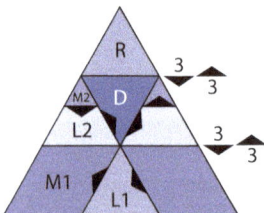

Magic wedge

1. Determine the best selection of a 3½″ R triangle set (see Cutting the Strips, page 18). After the shapes are cut, refer to Design Possibilities (page 18) for ideas on how the shapes can be rotated for different looks. When you've determined the best look for each set of shapes, mark the center so you can piece them together appropriately.

2. Using 1 R triangle, 1 L1 triangle, 2 M1 diamonds, 1 D triangle, and 2 L2-M2 strip-pieced triangles, arrange 1 wedge.

3. Sew the 2 M1 diamonds to the sides of the L1 triangle to make the lower unit.

4. Sew the 2 L2-M2 strip-pieced triangles to the D triangle to make the middle unit.

5. Attach the R triangle to the middle unit. Add the lower unit to complete 1 wedge.

6. Make 6 identical wedges.

7. Arrange the wedges into a hexagon, with the repeat fabric at the center.

8. Sew the wedges into groups of 3 to make half-hexagons. Then sew the center seam to complete the block. Refer to Sewing and Pressing Options (page 32) if needed.

48 STACK & CUT Hexagon Quilts

MIX & MATCH

Finished Mix & Match block: 11″ × 12¾″

These two blocks are smaller and simple for a great starting project. The yardage is for a design with nine blocks each of the two repeat fabrics, with coordinating fabrics being consistent throughout the quilt. Because of the smaller block size, you will not be able to use the standard setting triangles. Either design your quilt without setting triangles (see Blocks-Only Settings, page 98) or make setting triangles using a 6¼″ cut triangle.

If a variety of fabrics is desired, read Using Multiple Fabrics per Shape (page 23) to figure yardage. Refer to General Information for Making Blocks (page 32) as needed.

YARDAGE AND CUTTING

Cut the strips and corresponding shapes using the instructions on the pages noted in the table. Refer to Cutting the Strips (page 18) as needed.

FABRIC	YDG FOR 9 BLOCKS	STRIP QTY AND SIZE TO CUT FOR 9 BLOCKS	QTY, SHAPE, AND SIZE TO CUT FOR 9 BLOCKS	QTY OF SHAPE IN 1 BLOCK
REPEAT 1 HEXAGONS (R) (A set is 6 layers.)	Minimum of 24″ repeat or 4 yards	3 stacked strip sets 6¼″ × 20″	9 triangle sets 6¼″ (page 116)	1 set of 6
REPEAT 2 STARS (R) (A set is 6 layers.)	Minimum of 18″ repeat or 3 yards	3 stacked strip sets 3¼″ × 20″	9 diamond sets 3¼″ (page 117)	1 set of 6
LIGHT (L)	⅞ yard	6 strips 3½″ × WOF	108 triangles 3½″ (page 116)	12

Piecing

Review General Information for Making Blocks (page 32). Seam allowances are ¼″ unless otherwise noted. Follow the arrows for pressing directions.

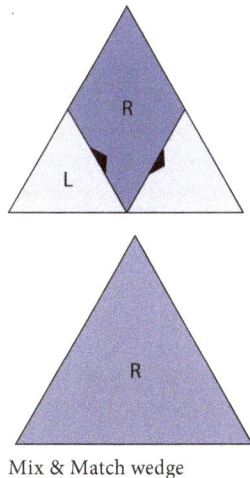

Mix & Match wedge

1. Determine the best selection of a 6¼″ R triangle set and a 3¼″ R diamond set (see Cutting the Strips, page 18). After the shapes are cut, refer to Design Possibilities (page 18) for ideas on how the shapes can be rotated for different looks. When you've determined the best look for each set of shapes, mark the center so you can piece them together appropriately.

2. Using 1 R diamond and 2 L triangles, arrange 1 wedge.

3. Sew the 2 L triangles to the non-center edges of the R diamond to complete 1 wedge.

4. Make 6 identical wedges.

5. Arrange the wedges into a hexagon, with the repeat fabric at the center.

6. Sew the wedges into groups of 3 to make half-hexagons. Then sew the center seam to complete the block. Refer to Sewing and Pressing Options (page 32) as needed.

7. Repeat only Steps 1 and 6 for the 6¼″ R triangles.

Block Designs

MOONGLOW

Finished Moonglow block: 16½″ × 19″

The following yardage is for up to nine blocks, with all the blocks created from the same fabrics. If a variety of fabrics is desired throughout the nine blocks, read Using Multiple Fabrics per Shape (page 23) to figure yardage. Refer to General Information for Making Blocks (page 32) as needed.

YARDAGE AND CUTTING

Cut the strips and corresponding shapes using the instructions on the pages noted in the table. Refer to Cutting the Strips (page 18) as needed.

FABRIC	YDG FOR 9 BLOCKS	STRIP QTY AND SIZE TO CUT FOR 9 BLOCKS	QTY, SHAPE, AND SIZE TO CUT FOR 9 BLOCKS	QTY OF SHAPE IN 1 BLOCK
REPEAT (R) (A set is 6 layers.)	Minimum of 15″ repeat or 2½ yards	2 stacked strip sets 4⅞″ × 20″	9 triangle sets 4⅞″ (page 116)	1 set of 6
LIGHT (L)	⅞ yard	10 strips 2⅝″ × WOF	108 strip-pieced triangles 4⅞″ (page 116)	12
MEDIUM (M)	⅝ yard	5 strips 2¾″ × WOF		
DARK (D)	1 yard	5 strips 4⅞″ × WOF	54 triangles 4⅞″ (page 116)	6

Piecing

Review General Information for Making Blocks (page 32). Seam allowances are ¼″ unless otherwise noted. Follow the arrows for pressing directions.

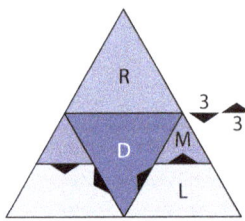

Moonglow wedge

1. Determine the best selection of a 4⅞″ R triangle set (see Cutting the Strips, page 18). After the shapes are cut, refer to Design Possibilities (page 18) for ideas on how the shapes can be rotated for different looks. When you've determined the best look for each set of shapes, mark the center so you can piece them together appropriately.

2. Using 1 R triangle, 1 D triangle, and 2 L-M strip-pieced triangles, arrange 1 wedge.

3. Sew the 2 L-M strip-pieced triangles on either side of the D triangle.

4. Attach the R triangle to complete 1 wedge.

5. Make 6 identical wedges.

6. Arrange the wedges into a hexagon, with the repeat fabric at the center.

7. Sew the wedges into groups of 3 to make half-hexagons. Then sew the center seam to complete the block. Refer to Sewing and Pressing Options (page 32) as needed.

ORNAMENT

Finished Ornament block: 16½˝ × 19˝

The following yardage is for up to nine blocks, with all the blocks created from the same fabrics. If a variety of fabrics is desired throughout the nine blocks, read Using Multiple Fabrics per Shape (page 23) to figure yardage. Refer to General Information for Making Blocks (page 32) as needed.

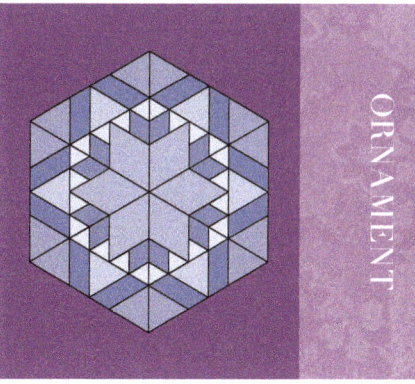

YARDAGE AND CUTTING

Cut the strips and corresponding shapes using the instructions on the pages noted in the table. Refer to Cutting the Strips (page 18) as needed.

FABRIC	YDG FOR 9 BLOCKS	STRIP QTY AND SIZE TO CUT FOR 9 BLOCKS	QTY, SHAPE, AND SIZE TO CUT FOR 9 BLOCKS	QTY OF SHAPE IN 1 BLOCK
REPEAT (R) (A set is 6 layers.)	Minimum of 18˝ repeat or 3 yards	3 stacked strip sets 3¼˝ × 20˝	9 diamond sets 3¼˝ (page 117)	1 set of 6
LIGHT 1 (L1)	½ yard	3 strips 3½˝ × WOF	54 triangles 3½˝ (page 116)	6
LIGHT 2 (L2)	⅝ yard	7 strips 2⅛˝ × WOF	216 triangles 2⅛˝ (page 116)	24
MEDIUM (M)	⅞ yard	6 strips 3½˝ × WOF	108 triangles 3½˝ (page 116)	12
DARK 1 (D1)	½ yard	7 strips 1⅞˝ × WOF	108 diamonds 1⅞˝ (page 117)	12
DARK 2 (D2)	¾ yard	11 strips 1⅞˝ × WOF	108 long diamonds 3¼˝ (54 L and 54 R) (page 118)	12 (6 L and 6 R)

Piecing

Review General Information for Making Blocks (page 32). Seam allowances are ¼˝ unless otherwise noted. Follow the arrows for pressing directions.

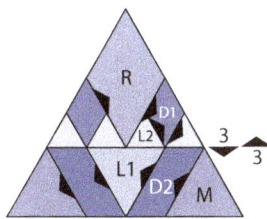

Ornament wedge

1. Determine the best selection of a 3¼˝ R diamond set (see Cutting the Strips, page 18). After the shapes are cut, refer to Design Possibilities (page 18) for ideas on how the shapes can be rotated for different looks. When you've determined the best look for each set of shapes, mark the center so you can piece them together appropriately.

2. Using 1 R diamond, 1 L1 triangle, 4 L2 triangles, 2 M triangles, 2 D1 diamonds, and 2 D2 long diamonds (1 left and 1 right), arrange 1 wedge.

3. Sew 2 L2 triangles to a D1 diamond. Repeat to make 2 units. Sew to the non-center edges of the R diamond to make the upper unit.

4. Sew the 2 D2 long diamonds to the M triangles so they are a mirror image, as shown. Sew to the L1 triangle to make the lower unit.

5. Join the upper and lower units to complete 1 wedge.

6. Make 6 identical wedges.

7. Arrange the wedges into a hexagon, with the repeat fabric at the center.

8. Sew the wedges into groups of 3 to make half-hexagons. Then sew the center seam to complete the block. Refer to Sewing and Pressing Options (page 32) as needed.

PARK PLACE

Finished Park Place block: 16½˝ × 19˝

The following yardage is for up to nine blocks, with all the blocks created from the same fabrics. If a variety of fabrics is desired throughout the nine blocks, read Using Multiple Fabrics per Shape (page 23) to figure yardage. Refer to General Information for Making Blocks (page 32) as needed.

YARDAGE AND CUTTING

Cut the strips and corresponding shapes using the instructions on the pages noted in the table. Refer to Cutting the Strips (page 18) as needed.

FABRIC	YDG FOR 9 BLOCKS	STRIP QTY AND SIZE TO CUT FOR 9 BLOCKS	QTY, SHAPE, AND SIZE TO CUT FOR 9 BLOCKS	QTY OF SHAPE IN 1 BLOCK
REPEAT (R) (A set is 6 layers.)	Minimum of 24˝ repeat or 4 yards	3 stacked strip sets 6¼˝ × 20˝	9 triangle sets 6¼˝ (page 116)	1 set of 6
LIGHT (L)	½ yard	3 strips 3½˝ × WOF	54 triangles 3½˝ (page 116)	6
DARK (D)	1¼ yards	11 strips 3¼˝ × WOF	108 diamonds 3¼˝ (page 117)	12

Piecing

Review General Information for Making Blocks (page 32). Seam allowances are ¼˝ unless otherwise noted. Follow the arrows for pressing directions.

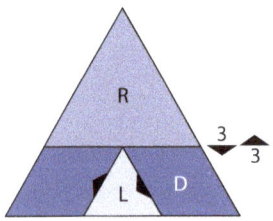

Park Place wedge

1. Determine the best selection of a 6¼˝ R triangle set (see Cutting the Strips, page 18). After the shapes are cut, refer to Design Possibilities (page 18) for ideas on how the shapes can be rotated for different looks. When you've determined the best look for each set of shapes, mark the center so you can piece them together appropriately.

2. Using 1 R triangle, 1 L triangle, and 2 D diamonds, arrange 1 wedge.

3. Sew the 2 D diamonds on either side of the L triangle. Attach the R triangle to complete 1 wedge.

4. Make 6 identical wedges.

5. Arrange the wedges into a hexagon, with the repeat fabric at the center.

6. Sew the wedges into groups of 3 to make half-hexagons. Then sew the center seam to complete the block. Refer to Sewing and Pressing Options (page 32) as needed.

PATRIOT

Finished Patriot block: 16½″ × 19″

The following yardage is for up to nine blocks, with all the blocks created from the same fabrics. If a variety of fabrics is desired throughout the nine blocks, read Using Multiple Fabrics per Shape (page 23) to figure yardage. Refer to General Information for Making Blocks (page 32) as needed.

YARDAGE AND CUTTING

Cut the strips and corresponding shapes using the instructions on the pages noted in the table. Refer to Cutting the Strips (page 18) as needed.

FABRIC	YDG FOR 9 BLOCKS	STRIP QTY AND SIZE TO CUT FOR 9 BLOCKS	QTY, SHAPE, AND SIZE TO CUT FOR 9 BLOCKS	QTY OF SHAPE IN 1 BLOCK
REPEAT (R) (A set is 6 layers.)	Minimum of 18″ repeat or 3 yards	3 stacked strip sets 3¼″ × 20″	9 diamond sets 3¼″ (page 117)	1 set of 6
LIGHT (L)	½ yard	3 strips 3½″ × WOF	54 triangles 3½″ (page 116)	6
MEDIUM (M)	⅞ yard	6 strips 3½″ × WOF	108 triangles 3½″ (page 116)	12
DARK (D)	1¼ yards	11 strips 3¼″ × WOF	108 flat pyramids 4⅞″ (page 121)	12

Piecing

Review General Information for Making Blocks (page 32). Seam allowances are ¼″ unless otherwise noted. Follow the arrows for pressing directions.

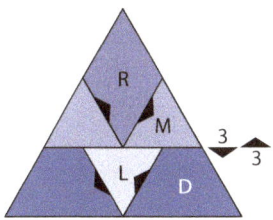

Patriot wedge

1. Determine the best selection of a 3¼″ R diamond set (see Cutting the Strips, page 18). After the shapes are cut, refer to Design Possibilities (page 18) for ideas on how the shapes can be rotated for different looks. When you've determined the best look for each set of shapes, mark the center so you can piece them together appropriately.

2. Using 1 R diamond, 1 L triangle, 2 M triangles, and 2 D flat pyramids, arrange 1 wedge.

3. Sew the 2 M triangles to the non-center edges of the R diamond to make the upper unit.

4. Sew the 2 D flat pyramids on either side of the L triangle to make the lower unit.

5. Join the upper and lower units to complete 1 wedge.

6. Make 6 identical wedges.

7. Arrange the wedges into a hexagon, with the repeat fabric at the center.

8. Sew the wedges into groups of 3 to make half-hexagons. Then sew the center seam to complete the block. Refer to Sewing and Pressing Options (page 32) as needed.

Block Designs

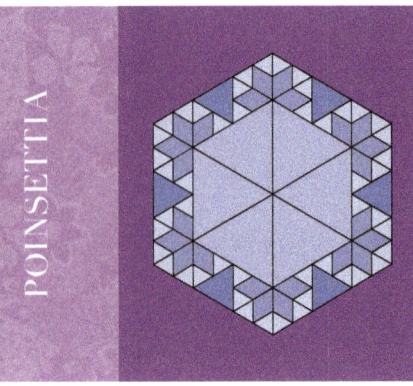

POINSETTIA

Finished Poinsettia block: 16½″ × 19″

The following yardage is for up to nine blocks, with all the blocks created from the same fabrics. If a variety of fabrics is desired throughout the nine blocks, read Using Multiple Fabrics per Shape (page 23) to figure yardage. Refer to General Information for Making Blocks (page 32) as needed.

YARDAGE AND CUTTING

Cut the strips and corresponding shapes using the instructions on the pages noted in the table. Refer to Cutting the Strips (page 18) as needed.

FABRIC	YDG FOR 9 BLOCKS	STRIP QTY AND SIZE TO CUT FOR 9 BLOCKS	QTY, SHAPE, AND SIZE TO CUT FOR 9 BLOCKS	QTY OF SHAPE IN 1 BLOCK
REPEAT (R) (A set is 6 layers.)	Minimum of 24″ repeat or 4 yards	3 stacked strip sets 6¼″ × 20″	9 triangle sets 6¼″ (page 116)	1 set of 6
LIGHT (L)	1 yard	14 strips 2⅛″ × WOF	432 triangles 2⅛″ (page 116)	48
MEDIUM (M)	⅞ yard	13 strips 1⅞″ × WOF	216 diamonds 1⅞″ (page 117)	24
DARK (D)	½ yard	3 strips 3½″ × WOF	54 triangles 3½″ (page 116)	6

Piecing

Review General Information for Making Blocks (page 32). Seam allowances are ¼″ unless otherwise noted. Follow the arrows for pressing directions.

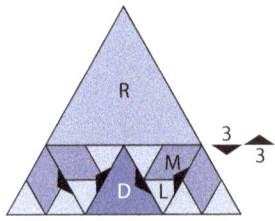

Poinsettia wedge

1. Determine the best selection of a 6¼″ R triangle set (see Cutting the Strips, page 18). After the shapes are cut, refer to Design Possibilities (page 18) for ideas on how the shapes can be rotated for different looks. When you've determined the best look for each set of shapes, mark the center so you can piece them together appropriately.

2. Using 1 R triangle, 8 L triangles, 4 M diamonds, and 1 D triangle, arrange 1 wedge.

3. Sew 2 L triangles on either side of 1 M diamond to make 1 triangle unit. Make 4 triangle units.

4. Join 2 triangle units together with their diamond points touching. Make 2. Sew to the D triangle so they are a mirror image, as shown.

5. Attach the R triangle to complete 1 wedge.

6. Make 6 identical wedges.

7. Arrange the wedges into a hexagon, with the repeat fabric at the center.

8. Sew the wedges into groups of 3 to make half-hexagons. Then sew the center seam to complete the block. Refer to Sewing and Pressing Options (page 32) as needed.

PORTHOLE

Finished Porthole block: 16½″ × 19″

The following yardage is for up to nine blocks, with all the blocks created from the same fabrics. If a variety of fabrics is desired throughout the nine blocks, read Using Multiple Fabrics per Shape (page 23) to figure yardage. Refer to General Information for Making Blocks (page 32) as needed.

YARDAGE AND CUTTING

Cut the strips and corresponding shapes using the instructions on the pages noted in the table. Refer to Cutting the Strips (page 18) as needed.

FABRIC	YDG FOR 9 BLOCKS	STRIP QTY AND SIZE TO CUT FOR 9 BLOCKS	QTY, SHAPE, AND SIZE TO CUT FOR 9 BLOCKS	QTY OF SHAPE IN 1 BLOCK
REPEAT (R) (A set is 6 layers.)	Minimum of 24″ repeat or 4 yards	3 stacked strip sets 6¼″ × 20″	9 triangle sets 6¼″ (page 116)	1 set of 6
MEDIUM (M)	1½ yards	14 strips 3¼″ × WOF	54 flat pyramids 9″ (page 121)	6

Piecing

Review General Information for Making Blocks (page 32). Seam allowances are ¼″ unless otherwise noted. Follow the arrows for pressing directions.

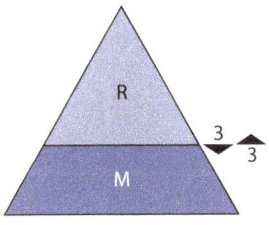

Porthole wedge

1. Determine the best selection of a 6¼″ R triangle set (see Cutting the Strips, page 18). After the shapes are cut, refer to Design Possibilities (page 18) for ideas on how the shapes can be rotated for different looks. When you've determined the best look for each set of shapes, mark the center so you can piece them together appropriately.

2. Using 1 R triangle and 1 M flat pyramid, arrange 1 wedge.

3. Attach the R triangle to the M flat pyramid to complete 1 wedge.

4. Make 6 identical wedges.

5. Arrange the wedges into a hexagon, with the repeat fabric at the center.

6. Sew the wedges into groups of 3 to make half-hexagons. Then sew the center seam to complete the block. Refer to Sewing and Pressing Options (page 32) as needed.

PRICKLY PEAR

Finished Prickly Pear block: 16½" × 19"

The following yardage is for up to nine blocks, with all the blocks created from the same fabrics. If a variety of fabrics is desired throughout the nine blocks, read Using Multiple Fabrics per Shape (page 23) to figure yardage. Refer to General Information for Making Blocks (page 32) as needed.

YARDAGE AND CUTTING

Cut the strips and corresponding shapes using the instructions on the pages noted in the table. Refer to Cutting the Strips (page 18) as needed.

FABRIC	YDG FOR 9 BLOCKS	STRIP QTY AND SIZE TO CUT FOR 9 BLOCKS	QTY, SHAPE, AND SIZE TO CUT FOR 9 BLOCKS	QTY OF SHAPE IN 1 BLOCK
REPEAT (R) (A set is 6 layers.)	Minimum of 20" repeat or 3½ yards	3 stacked strip sets 4⅝" × 20"	9 diamond sets 4⅝" (page 117)	1 set of 6
LIGHT (L)	½ yard	4 strips 2⅛" × WOF	108 triangles 2⅛" (page 116)	12
MEDIUM (M)	⅞ yard	6 strips 3½" × WOF	108 matched triangles 3½" (page 122)	12
DARK (D)	1⅛ yards	6 strips 3½" × WOF		
		3 strips 3½" × WOF	54 triangles 3½" (page 116)	6

Piecing

Review General Information for Making Blocks (page 32). Seam allowances are ¼" unless otherwise noted. Follow the arrows for pressing directions.

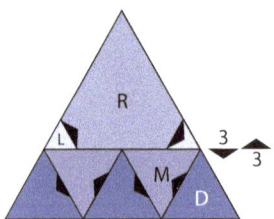

Prickly Pear wedge

1. Determine the best selection of a 4⅝" R diamond set (see Cutting the Strips, page 18). After the shapes are cut, refer to Design Possibilities (page 18) for ideas on how the shapes can be rotated for different looks. When you've determined the best look for each set of shapes, mark the center so you can piece them together appropriately. On the other end, trim off a 3" triangle to make the gem shape (page 121).

2. Using 1 R gem shape, 2 L triangles, 2 M-D matched triangles, and 1 D triangle, arrange 1 wedge.

3. Sew the 2 L triangles to the sides of the R gem shape to make the upper unit.

4. Sew the M-D matched triangles to the D triangle to make the lower unit.

5. Join the upper and lower units to complete 1 wedge.

6. Make 6 identical wedges.

7. Arrange the wedges into a hexagon, with the repeat fabric at the center.

8. Sew the wedges into groups of 3 to make half-hexagons. Then sew the center seam to complete the block. Refer to Sewing and Pressing Options (page 32) as needed.

RINGSTONE

Finished Ringstone block: 16½″ × 19″

The following yardage is for up to nine blocks, with all the blocks created from the same fabrics. If a variety of fabrics is desired throughout the nine blocks, read Using Multiple Fabrics per Shape (page 23) to figure yardage. Refer to General Information for Making Blocks (page 32) as needed.

YARDAGE AND CUTTING

Cut the strips and corresponding shapes using the instructions on the pages noted in the table. Refer to Cutting the Strips (page 18) as needed.

FABRIC	YDG FOR 9 BLOCKS	STRIP QTY AND SIZE TO CUT FOR 9 BLOCKS	QTY, SHAPE, AND SIZE TO CUT FOR 9 BLOCKS	QTY OF SHAPE IN 1 BLOCK
REPEAT (R) (A set is 6 layers.)	Minimum of 18″ repeat or 3 yards	3 stacked strip sets 3¼″ × 20″	9 diamond sets 3¼″ (page 117)	1 set of 6
LIGHT 1 (L1)	¾ yard	11 strips 1⅞″ × WOF	108 strip-pieced diamonds 3¼″ (54 L and 54 R) (page 120)	12 (6 L and 6 R)
DARK (D)	¾ yard	11 strips 1⅞″ × WOF		
LIGHT 2 (L2)	½ yard	3 strips 3½″ × WOF	54 triangles 3½″ (page 116)	6
MEDIUM (M)	⅞ yard	6 strips 3½″ × WOF	108 triangles 3½″ (page 116)	12

Piecing

Review General Information for Making Blocks (page 32). Seam allowances are ¼″ unless otherwise noted. Follow the arrows for pressing directions.

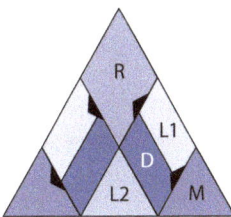

Ringstone wedge

1. Determine the best selection of a 3¼″ R diamond set (see Cutting the Strips, page 18). After the shapes are cut, refer to Design Possibilities (page 18) for ideas on how the shapes can be rotated for different looks. When you've determined the best look for each set of shapes, mark the center so you can piece them together appropriately.

2. Using 1 R diamond, 2 L1-D strip-pieced diamonds, 1 L2 triangle, and 2 M triangles, arrange 1 wedge.

3. Sew 1 R diamond to 1 L1-D strip-pieced diamond. Add 1 M triangle to make the long unit on the left.

4. Sew 1 L1-D strip-pieced diamond to a L2 triangle to make the short unit on the right.

5. Join the short and long units. Add the remaining M triangle on the lower right to complete 1 wedge.

6. Make 6 identical wedges.

7. Arrange the wedges into a hexagon, with the repeat fabric at the center.

8. Sew the wedges into groups of 3 to make half-hexagons. Then sew the center seam to complete the block. Refer to Sewing and Pressing Options (page 32) as needed.

RIPPLES

Finished Ripples block: 16½˝ × 19˝

The following yardage is for up to nine blocks, with all the blocks created from the same fabrics. If a variety of fabrics is desired throughout the nine blocks, read Using Multiple Fabrics per Shape (page 23) to figure yardage. Refer to General Information for Making Blocks (page 32) as needed.

YARDAGE AND CUTTING

Cut the strips and corresponding shapes using the instructions on the pages noted in the table. Refer to Cutting the Strips (page 18) as needed.

FABRIC	YDG FOR 9 BLOCKS	STRIP QTY AND SIZE TO CUT FOR 9 BLOCKS	QTY, SHAPE, AND SIZE TO CUT FOR 9 BLOCKS	QTY OF SHAPE IN 1 BLOCK
REPEAT (R) (A set is 6 layers.)	Minimum of 18˝ repeat or 3 yards	2 stacked strip sets 3½˝ × 20˝	9 triangle sets 3½˝ (page 116)	1 set of 6
LIGHT 1 (L1)	½ yard	3 strips 3½˝ × WOF	54 triangles 3½˝ (page 116)	6
LIGHT 2 (L2)	1 yard	8 strips 3¼˝ × WOF	54 flat pyramids 6¼˝ (page 121)	6
MEDIUM (M)	⅞ yard	6 strips 3½˝ × WOF	108 triangle 3½˝ (page 116)	12
DARK (D)	⅞ yard	6 strips 3½˝ × WOF	108 triangles 3½˝ (page 116)	12

Piecing

Review General Information for Making Blocks (page 32). Seam allowances are ¼˝ unless otherwise noted. Follow the arrows for pressing directions.

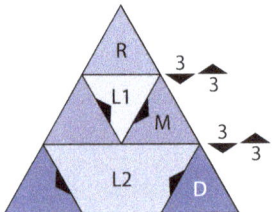

Ripples wedge

1. Determine the best selection of a 3½˝ repeat triangle set (see Cutting the Strips, page 18). After the shapes are cut, refer to Design Possibilities (page 18) for ideas on how the shapes can be rotated for different looks. When you've determined the best look for each set of shapes, mark the center so you can piece them together appropriately.

2. Using 1 R triangle, 1 L1 triangle, 2 M triangles, 1 L2 flat pyramid, and 2 D triangles, arrange 1 wedge.

3. Sew the 2 M triangles on either side of the L1 triangle. Attach the R triangle to make the upper unit.

4. Sew the 2 D triangles to either side of the L2 flat pyramid to make the lower unit.

5. Join the upper and lower units to complete 1 wedge.

6. Make 6 identical wedges.

7. Arrange the wedges into a hexagon, with the repeat fabric at the center.

8. Sew the wedges into groups of 3 to make half-hexagons. Then sew the center seam to complete the block. Refer to Sewing and Pressing Options (page 32) as needed.

ROSE WINDOW

Finished Rose Window block: 16½˝ × 19˝

The following yardage is for up to nine blocks, with all the blocks created from the same fabrics. If a variety of fabrics is desired throughout the nine blocks, read Using Multiple Fabrics per Shape (page 23) to figure yardage. Refer to General Information for Making Blocks (page 32) as needed.

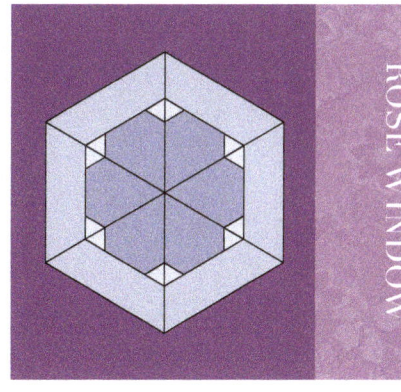

YARDAGE AND CUTTING

Cut the strips and corresponding shapes using the instructions on the pages noted in the table. Refer to Cutting the Strips (page 18) as needed.

FABRIC	YDG FOR 9 BLOCKS	STRIP QTY AND SIZE TO CUT FOR 9 BLOCKS	QTY, SHAPE, AND SIZE TO CUT FOR 9 BLOCKS	QTY OF SHAPE IN 1 BLOCK
REPEAT (R) (A set is 6 layers.)	Minimum of 20˝ repeat or 3½ yards	3 stacked strip sets 4⅝˝ × 20˝	9 diamond sets 4⅝˝ (page 117)	1 set of 6
LIGHT (L)	½ yard	4 strips 2⅛˝ × WOF	108 triangles 2⅛˝ (page 116)	12
MEDIUM (M)	1½ yards	14 strips 3¼˝ × WOF	54 flat pyramids 9˝ (page 121)	6

Piecing

Review General Information for Making Blocks (page 32). Seam allowances are ¼˝ unless otherwise noted. Follow the arrows for pressing directions.

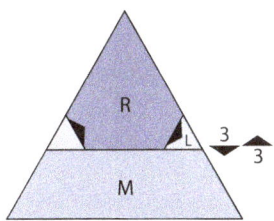

Rose Window wedge

1. Determine the best selection of a 4⅝˝ R diamond set (see Cutting the Strips, page 18). After the shapes are cut, refer to Design Possibilities (page 18) for ideas on how the shapes can be rotated for different looks. When you've determined the best look for each set of shapes, mark the center so you can piece them together appropriately. On the other end, trim off a 3˝ triangle to make the gem shape (page 121).

2. Using 1 R gem shape, 2 L triangles, and 1 M flat pyramid, arrange 1 wedge.

3. Sew the 2 L triangles to the sides of the R gem shape.

4. Add the M flat pyramid to complete 1 wedge.

5. Make 6 identical wedges.

6. Arrange the wedges into a hexagon, with the repeat fabric at the center.

7. Sew the wedges into groups of 3 to make half-hexagons. Then sew the center seam to complete the block. Refer to Sewing and Pressing Options (page 32) as needed.

SAILOR'S DREAM

Finished Sailor's Dream block: 16½″ × 19″

The following yardage is for up to nine blocks, with all the blocks created from the same fabrics. If a variety of fabrics is desired throughout the nine blocks, read Using Multiple Fabrics per Shape (page 23) to figure yardage. Refer to General Information for Making Blocks (page 32) as needed.

YARDAGE AND CUTTING

Cut the strips and corresponding shapes using the instructions on the pages noted in the table. Refer to Cutting the Strips (page 18) as needed.

FABRIC	YDG FOR 9 BLOCKS	STRIP QTY AND SIZE TO CUT FOR 9 BLOCKS	QTY, SHAPE, AND SIZE TO CUT FOR 9 BLOCKS	QTY OF SHAPE IN 1 BLOCK
REPEAT (R) (A set is 6 layers.)	Minimum of 18″ repeat or 3 yards	2 stacked strip sets 3½″ × 20″	9 triangle sets 3½″ (page 116)	1 set of 6
LIGHT 1 (L1)	⅞ yard	12 strips 1⅞″ × WOF	108 strip-pieced triangles 3½″ (page 116)	12
MEDIUM 1 (M1)	½ yard	6 strips 2⅛″ × WOF		
LIGHT 2 (L2)	½ yard	4 strips 2⅛″ × WOF	108 triangles 2⅛″ (page 116)	12
LIGHT 3 (L3)	⅝ yard	9 strips 1⅞″ × WOF	108 flat pyramids 3½″ (page 121)	12
MEDIUM 2 (M2)	½ yard	4 strips 2⅛″ × WOF	108 triangles 2⅛″ (page 116)	12
MEDIUM 3 (M3)	⅞ yard	6 strips 3½″ × WOF	108 triangles 3½″ (page 116)	12
DARK 1 (D1)	½ yard	3 strips 3½″ × WOF	54 triangles 3½″ (page 116)	6
DARK 2 (D2)	⅜ yard	4 strips 1⅞″ × WOF	54 diamonds 1⅞″ (page 117)	6

Piecing

Review General Information for Making Blocks (page 32). Seam allowances are ¼″ unless otherwise noted. Follow the arrows for pressing directions.

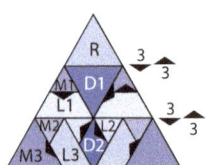

Sailor's Dream wedge

1. Determine the best selection of a 3½″ R triangle set (see Cutting the Strips, page 18). After the shapes are cut, refer to Design Possibilities (page 18) for ideas on how the shapes can be rotated for different looks. Mark the center to piece them together appropriately.

2. Using 1 R triangle, 2 L1-M1 strip-pieced triangles, 2 L2 triangles, 2 L3 flat pyramids, 2 M2 triangles, 2 M3 triangles, 1 D1 triangle, and 1 D2 diamond, arrange 1 wedge.

3. Sew 2 L1-M1 triangles to 1 D1 triangle. Attach 1 R triangle to make the upper unit.

4. Sew 2 L2 triangles on either side of 1 D2 diamond to make a triangle unit.

5. Sew 2 M2 triangles to 2 L3 pyramids so they are a mirror image.

6. Sew 2 mirror-image units to 1 triangle unit. Add 2 M3 triangles to make the lower unit.

7. Join the upper and lower units to complete 1 wedge.

8. Make 6 identical wedges.

9. Arrange the wedges with the R triangles at the center.

10. Sew the wedges into groups of 3 to make half-hexagons. Sew the center seam to complete the block. Refer to Sewing and Pressing Options (page 32) as needed.

SAILOR'S STAR

Finished Sailor's Star block: 16½" × 19"

The following yardage is for up to nine blocks, with all the blocks created from the same fabrics. If a variety of fabrics is desired throughout the nine blocks, read Using Multiple Fabrics per Shape (page 23) to figure yardage. Refer to General Information for Making Blocks (page 32) as needed.

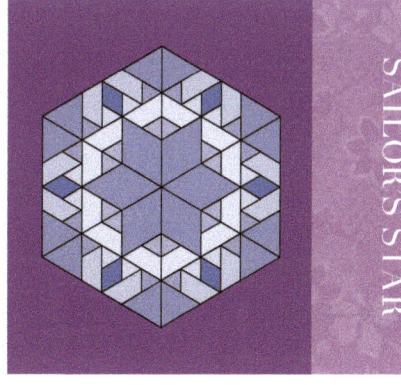

YARDAGE AND CUTTING

Cut the strips and corresponding shapes using the instructions on the pages noted in the table. Refer to Cutting the Strips (page 18) as needed.

FABRIC	YDG FOR 9 BLOCKS	STRIP QTY AND SIZE TO CUT FOR 9 BLOCKS	QTY, SHAPE, AND SIZE TO CUT FOR 9 BLOCKS	QTY OF SHAPE IN 1 BLOCK
REPEAT (R) (A set is 6 layers.)	Minimum of 18" repeat or 3 yards	3 stacked strip sets 3¼" × 20"	9 diamond sets 3¼" (page 117)	1 set of 6
LIGHT 1 (L1)	⅞ yard	12 strips 1⅞" × WOF	108 strip-pieced triangles 3½" (page 116)	12
MEDIUM 1 (M1)	½ yard	6 strips 2⅛" × WOF		
LIGHT 2 (L2)	½ yard	4 strips 2⅛" × WOF	108 triangles 2⅛" (page 116)	12
LIGHT 3 (L3)	⅝ yard	9 strips 1⅞" × WOF	108 flat pyramids 3½" (page 121)	12
MEDIUM 2 (M2)	½ yard	4 strips 2⅛" × WOF	108 triangles 2⅛" (page 116)	12
MEDIUM 3 (M3)	⅞ yard	6 strips 3½" × WOF	108 triangles 3½" (page 116)	12
DARK (D)	⅜ yard	4 strips 1⅞" × WOF	54 diamonds 1⅞" (page 117)	6

Piecing

Review General Information for Making Blocks (page 32). Seam allowances are ¼" unless otherwise noted. Follow the arrows for pressing directions.

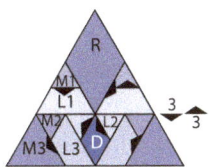

Sailor's Star wedge

1. Determine the best selection of a 3¼" R diamond set (see Cutting the Strips, page 18). After the shapes are cut, refer to Design Possibilities (page 18) for ideas on how the shapes can be rotated for different looks. Mark the center so you can piece them together appropriately.

2. Using 1 R diamond, 2 L1-M1 strip-pieced triangles, 2 L2 triangles, 2 L3 flat pyramids, 2 M2 triangles, 2 M3 triangles, and 1 D diamond, arrange 1 wedge.

3. Sew 2 L1-M1 triangles to the non-center edges of 1 R diamond to make the upper unit.

4. Sew the 2 L2 triangles to 1 D diamond to make a triangle unit.

5. Sew 2 M2 triangles to 2 L3 flat pyramids so they are a mirror image, as shown.

6. Sew 2 mirror-image units to the triangle unit's sides. Add 2 M3 triangles to make the lower unit.

7. Join the upper and lower units to complete 1 wedge.

8. Make 6 identical wedges.

9. Arrange the wedges with the R diamonds at the center.

10. Sew the wedges into groups of 3 to make half-hexagons. Sew the center seam to complete the block. Refer to Sewing and Pressing Options (page 32) as needed.

SHY EYES

Finished Shy Eyes block: 16½″ × 19″

The following yardage is for up to nine blocks, with all the blocks created from the same fabrics. If a variety of fabrics is desired throughout the nine blocks, read Using Multiple Fabrics per Shape (page 23) to figure yardage. Refer to General Information for Making Blocks (page 32) as needed.

YARDAGE AND CUTTING

Cut the strips and corresponding shapes using the instructions on the pages noted in the table. Refer to Cutting the Strips (page 18) as needed.

FABRIC	YDG FOR 9 BLOCKS	STRIP QTY AND SIZE TO CUT FOR 9 BLOCKS	QTY, SHAPE, AND SIZE TO CUT FOR 9 BLOCKS	QTY OF SHAPE IN 1 BLOCK
REPEAT (R) (A set is 6 layers.)	Minimum of 24″ repeat or 4 yards	3 stacked strip sets 6¼″ × 20″	9 triangle sets 6¼″ (page 116)	1 set of 6
LIGHT 1 (L1)	½ yard	3 strips 3½″ × WOF	54 triangles 3½″ (page 116)	6
LIGHT 2 (L2)	⅝ yard	7 strips 2⅛″ × WOF	216 matched triangles 2⅛″ (page 122)	24
DARK (D)	⅝ yard	7 strips 2⅛″ × WOF		
MEDIUM (M)	⅞ yard	6 strips 3½″ × WOF	108 triangles 3½″ (page 116)	12

Piecing

Review General Information for Making Blocks (page 32). Seam allowances are ¼″ unless otherwise noted. Follow the arrows for pressing directions.

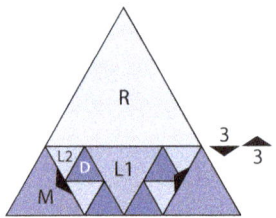

Shy Eyes wedge

1. Determine the best selection of a 6¼″ R triangle set (see Cutting the Strips, page 18). After the shapes are cut, refer to Design Possibilities (page 18) for ideas on how the shapes can be rotated for different looks. When you've determined the best look for each set of shapes, mark the center so you can piece them together appropriately.

2. Using 1 R triangle, 1 L1 triangle, 4 L2-D matched triangles, and 2 M triangles, arrange 1 wedge.

3. Sew the L2-D matched triangles together so they are a mirror image, as shown.

4. Sew the mirror-image units to the L1 triangle. Add the M triangles to the ends. Attach the R triangle to complete 1 wedge.

5. Make 6 identical wedges.

6. Arrange the wedges into a hexagon, with the repeat fabric at the center.

7. Sew the wedges into groups of 3 to make half-hexagons. Then sew the center seam to complete the block. Refer to Sewing and Pressing Options (page 32) as needed.

SONATA

Finished Sonata block: 16½″ × 19″

The following yardage is for up to nine blocks, with all the blocks created from the same fabrics. If a variety of fabrics is desired throughout the nine blocks, read Using Multiple Fabrics per Shape (page 23) to figure yardage. Refer to General Information for Making Blocks (page 32) as needed.

YARDAGE AND CUTTING

Cut the strips and corresponding shapes using the instructions on the pages noted in the table. Refer to Cutting the Strips (page 18) as needed.

FABRIC	YDG FOR 9 BLOCKS	STRIP QTY AND SIZE TO CUT FOR 9 BLOCKS	QTY, SHAPE, AND SIZE TO CUT FOR 9 BLOCKS	QTY OF SHAPE IN 1 BLOCK
REPEAT (R) (A set is 6 layers.)	Minimum of 24″ repeat or 4 yards	3 stacked strip sets 6¼″ × 20″	9 triangle sets 6¼″ (page 116)	1 set of 6
MEDIUM (M)	1 yard	8 strips 3¼″ × WOF	54 flat pyramids 6¼″ (page 121)	6
DARK (D)	⅞ yard	6 strips 3½″ × WOF	108 triangles 3½″ (page 116)	12

Piecing

Review General Information for Making Blocks (page 32). Seam allowances are ¼″ unless otherwise noted. Follow the arrows for pressing directions.

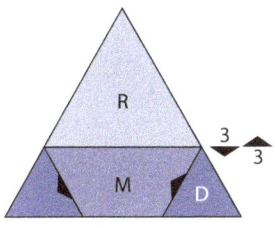

Sonata wedge

1. Determine the best selection of a 6¼″ R triangle set (see Cutting the Strips, page 18). After the shapes are cut, refer to Design Possibilities (page 18) for ideas on how the shapes can be rotated for different looks. When you've determined the best look for each set of shapes, mark the center so you can piece them together appropriately.

2. Using 1 R triangle, 1 M flat pyramid, and 2 D triangles, arrange 1 wedge.

3. Sew the 2 D triangles on either side of the M flat pyramid.

4. Attach the R triangle to complete 1 wedge.

5. Make 6 identical wedges.

6. Arrange the wedges into a hexagon, with the repeat fabric at the center.

7. Sew the wedges into groups of 3 to make half-hexagons. Then sew the center seam to complete the block. Refer to Sewing and Pressing Options (page 32) as needed.

STAINED GLASS

Finished Stained Glass block: 16½″ × 19″

The following yardage is for up to nine blocks, with all the blocks created from the same fabrics. If a variety of fabrics is desired throughout the nine blocks, read Using Multiple Fabrics per Shape (page 23) to figure yardage. Refer to General Information for Making Blocks (page 32) as needed.

YARDAGE AND CUTTING

Cut the strips and corresponding shapes using the instructions on the pages noted in the table. Refer to Cutting the Strips (page 18) as needed.

FABRIC	YDG FOR 9 BLOCKS	STRIP QTY AND SIZE TO CUT FOR 9 BLOCKS	QTY, SHAPE, AND SIZE TO CUT FOR 9 BLOCKS	QTY OF SHAPE IN 1 BLOCK
REPEAT (R) (A set is 6 layers.)	Minimum of 20″ repeat or 3½ yards	3 stacked strip sets 4⅝″ × 20″	9 diamond sets 4⅝″ (page 117)	1 set of 6
LIGHT 1 (L1)	½ yard	4 strips 2⅛″ × WOF	108 triangles 2⅛″ (page 116)	12
LIGHT 2 (L2)	½ yard	3 strips 3½″ × WOF	54 triangles 3½″ (page 116)	6
MEDIUM (M)	⅞ yard	6 strips 3½″ × WOF	108 triangles 3½″ (page 116)	12
DARK (D)	¾ yard	11 strips 1⅞″ × WOF	108 long diamonds 3¼″ (54 L and 54 R) (page 118)	12 (6 L and 6 R)

Piecing

Review General Information for Making Blocks (page 32). Seam allowances are ¼″ unless otherwise noted. Follow the arrows for pressing directions.

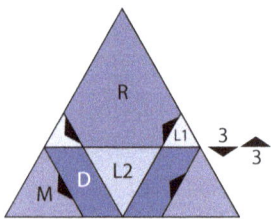

Stained Glass wedge

1. Determine the best selection of a 4⅝″ R diamond set (see Cutting the Strips, page 18). After the shapes are cut, refer to Design Possibilities (page 18) for ideas on how the shapes can be rotated for different looks. When you've determined the best look for each set of shapes, mark the center so you can piece them together appropriately. On the other end, trim off a 3″ triangle to make the gem shape (page 121).

2. Using 1 R gem shape, 2 L1 triangles, 1 L2 triangle, 2 M triangles, and 2 D long diamonds (1 left and 1 right), arrange 1 wedge.

3. Sew the 2 L1 triangles to the sides of the R gem shape to make the upper unit.

4. Sew the 2 D long diamonds on either side of the L2 triangle. Add 2 M triangles on the ends to make the lower unit.

5. Join the upper and lower units to complete 1 wedge.

6. Make 6 identical wedges.

7. Arrange the wedges into a hexagon, with the repeat fabric at the center.

8. Sew the wedges into groups of 3 to make half-hexagons. Then sew the center seam to complete the block. Refer to Sewing and Pressing Options (page 32) as needed.

STARRY PATH

Finished Starry Path block: 16½˝ × 19˝

The following yardage is for up to nine blocks, with all the blocks created from the same fabrics. If a variety of fabrics is desired throughout the nine blocks, read Using Multiple Fabrics per Shape (page 23) to figure yardage. Refer to General Information for Making Blocks (page 32) as needed.

YARDAGE AND CUTTING

Cut the strips and corresponding shapes using the instructions on the pages noted in the table. Refer to Cutting the Strips (page 18) as needed.

FABRIC	YDG FOR 9 BLOCKS	STRIP QTY AND SIZE TO CUT FOR 9 BLOCKS	QTY, SHAPE, AND SIZE TO CUT FOR 9 BLOCKS	QTY OF SHAPE IN 1 BLOCK
REPEAT (R) (A set is 6 layers.)	Minimum of 18˝ repeat or 3 yards	2 stacked strip sets 3½˝ × 20˝	9 triangle sets 3½˝ (page 116)	1 set of 6
LIGHT 1 (L1)	½ yard	3 strips 3½˝ × WOF	54 triangles 3½˝ (page 116)	6
LIGHT 2 (L2)	½ yard	3 strips 3½˝ × WOF	54 triangles 3½˝ (page 116)	6
MEDIUM (M)	⅞ yard	6 strips 3½˝ × WOF	108 triangles 3½˝ (page 116)	12
DARK (D)	1¼ yards	11 strips 3¼˝ × WOF	108 diamonds 3¼˝ (page 117)	12

Piecing

Review General Information for Making Blocks (page 32). Seam allowances are ¼˝ unless otherwise noted. Follow the arrows for pressing directions.

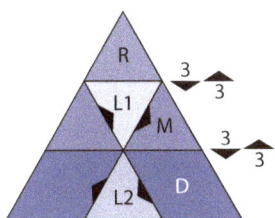

Starry Path wedge

1. Determine the best selection of a 3½˝ R triangle set (see Cutting the Strips, page 18). After the shapes are cut, refer to Design Possibilities (page 18) for ideas on how the shapes can be rotated for different looks. When you've determined the best look for each set of shapes, mark the center so you can piece them together appropriately.

2. Using 1 R triangle, 1 L1 triangle, 1 L2 triangle, 2 M triangles, and 2 D diamonds, arrange 1 wedge.

3. Sew the 2 M triangles on either side of the L1 triangle. Attach the R triangle to make the upper unit.

4. Sew the 2 D diamonds on either side of the L2 triangle to make the lower unit.

5. Join the upper and lower units to complete 1 wedge.

6. Make 6 identical wedges.

7. Arrange the wedges into a hexagon, with the repeat fabric at the center.

8. Sew the wedges into groups of 3 to make half-hexagons. Then sew the center seam to complete the block. Refer to Sewing and Pressing Options (page 32) as needed.

STARSTRUCK

Finished Starstruck block: 16½″ × 19″

The following yardage is for up to nine blocks, with all the blocks created from the same fabrics. If a variety of fabrics is desired throughout the nine blocks, read Using Multiple Fabrics per Shape (page 23) to figure yardage. Refer to General Information for Making Blocks (page 32) as needed.

YARDAGE AND CUTTING

Cut the strips and corresponding shapes using the instructions on the pages noted in the table. Refer to Cutting the Strips (page 18) as needed.

FABRIC	YDG FOR 9 BLOCKS	STRIP QTY AND SIZE TO CUT FOR 9 BLOCKS	QTY, SHAPE, AND SIZE TO CUT FOR 9 BLOCKS	QTY OF SHAPE IN 1 BLOCK
REPEAT (R) (A set is 6 layers.)	Minimum of 18″ repeat or 3 yards	3 stacked strip sets 3¼″ × 20″	9 diamond sets 3¼″ (page 117)	1 set of 6
LIGHT (L)	⅞ yard	12 strips 1⅞″ × WOF	108 strip-pieced triangles 3½″ (page 116)	12
DARK 1 (D1)	½ yard	6 strips 2⅛″ × WOF		
MEDIUM 1 (M1)	1¼ yards	11 strips 3¼″ × WOF	108 diamonds 3¼″ (page 117)	12
MEDIUM 2 (M2)	¼ yard	3 strips 2⅛″ × WOF	54 strip-pieced triangles 3½″ (page 116)	6
DARK 2 (D2)	½ yard	6 strips 1⅞″ × WOF		

Piecing

Review General Information for Making Blocks (page 32). Seam allowances are ¼″ unless otherwise noted. Follow the arrows for pressing directions.

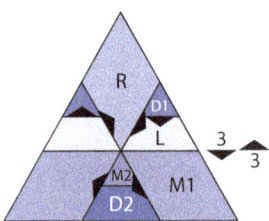

Starstruck wedge

1. Determine the best selection of a 3¼″ R diamond set (see Cutting the Strips, page 18). After the shapes are cut, refer to Design Possibilities (page 18) for ideas on how the shapes can be rotated for different looks. When you've determined the best look for each set of shapes, mark the center so you can piece them together appropriately.

2. Using 1 R diamond, 2 L-D1 strip-pieced triangles, 1 M2-D2 strip-pieced triangle, and 2 M1 diamonds, arrange 1 wedge.

3. Sew the 2 L-D1 strip-pieced triangles to the non-center edges of the R diamond to make the upper unit.

4. Sew the 2 M1 diamonds to either side of the M2-D2 strip-pieced triangle to make the lower unit.

5. Join the upper and lower units to complete 1 wedge.

6. Make 6 identical wedges.

7. Arrange the wedges into a hexagon, with the repeat fabric at the center.

8. Sew the wedges into groups of 3 to make half-hexagons. Then sew the center seam to complete the block. Refer to Sewing and Pressing Options (page 32) as needed.

SUSAN

Finished Susan block: 16½″ × 19″

The following yardage is for up to nine blocks, with all the blocks created from the same fabrics. If a variety of fabrics is desired throughout the nine blocks, read Using Multiple Fabrics per Shape (page 23) to figure yardage. Refer to General Information for Making Blocks (page 32) as needed.

YARDAGE AND CUTTING

Cut the strips and corresponding shapes using the instructions on the pages noted in the table. Refer to Cutting the Strips (page 18) as needed.

FABRIC	YDG FOR 9 BLOCKS	STRIP QTY AND SIZE TO CUT FOR 9 BLOCKS	QTY, SHAPE, AND SIZE TO CUT FOR 9 BLOCKS	QTY OF SHAPE IN 1 BLOCK
REPEAT (R) (A set is 6 layers.)	Minimum of 24″ repeat or 4 yards	3 stacked strip sets 6¼″ × 20″	9 triangle sets 6¼″ (page 116)	1 set of 6
LIGHT (L)	½ yard	3 strips 3½″ × WOF	54 triangles 3½″ (page 116)	6
MEDIUM (M)	⅞ yard	6 strips 3½″ × WOF	108 matched triangles 3½″ (page 122)	12
DARK (D)	⅞ yard	6 strips 3½″ × WOF		

Piecing

Review General Information for Making Blocks (page 32). Seam allowances are ¼″ unless otherwise noted. Follow the arrows for pressing directions.

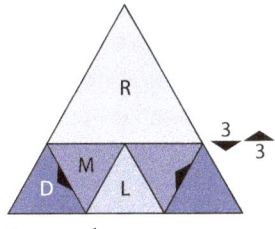

Susan wedge

1. Determine the best selection of a 6¼″ R triangle set (see Cutting the Strips, page 18). After the shapes are cut, refer to Design Possibilities (page 18) for ideas on how the shapes can be rotated for different looks. When you've determined the best look for each set of shapes, mark the center so you can piece them together appropriately.

2. Using 1 R triangle, 1 L triangle, and 2 M-D matched triangles, arrange 1 wedge.

3. Sew the 2 M-D matched triangles to either side of the L triangle so they are a mirror image, as shown.

4. Attach the R triangle to complete 1 wedge.

5. Make 6 identical wedges.

6. Arrange the wedges into a hexagon, with the repeat fabric at the center.

7. Sew the wedges into groups of 3 to make half-hexagons. Then sew the center seam to complete the block. Refer to Sewing and Pressing Options (page 32) as needed.

TICKTOCK

Finished Ticktock block: 16½″ × 19″

The following yardage is for up to nine blocks, with all the blocks created from the same fabrics. If a variety of fabrics is desired throughout the nine blocks, read Using Multiple Fabrics per Shape (page 23) to figure yardage. Refer to General Information for Making Blocks (page 32) as needed.

YARDAGE AND CUTTING

Cut the strips and corresponding shapes using the instructions on the pages noted in the table. Refer to Cutting the Strips (page 18) as needed.

FABRIC	YDG FOR 9 BLOCKS	STRIP QTY AND SIZE TO CUT FOR 9 BLOCKS	QTY, SHAPE, AND SIZE TO CUT FOR 9 BLOCKS	QTY OF SHAPE IN 1 BLOCK
REPEAT (R) (A set is 6 layers.)	Minimum of 24″ repeat or 4 yards	3 stacked strip sets 6¼″ × 20″	9 triangle sets 6¼″ (page 116)	1 set of 6
LIGHT (L)	⅝ yard	9 strips 1⅞″ × WOF	108 flat pyramids 3½″ (page 121)	12
MEDIUM (M)	⅝ yard	8 strips 2⅛″ × WOF	216 triangles 2⅛″ (page 116)	24
DARK 1 (D1)	⅜ yard	4 strips 1⅞″ × WOF	54 diamonds 1⅞″ (page 117)	6
DARK 2 (D2)	⅞ yard	6 strips 3½″ × WOF	108 triangles 3½″ (page 116)	12

Piecing

Review General Information for Making Blocks (page 32). Seam allowances are ¼″ unless otherwise noted. Follow the arrows for pressing directions.

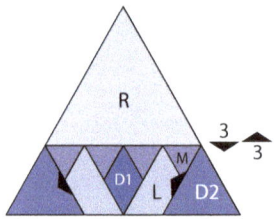

Ticktock wedge

1. Determine the best selection of a 6¼″ R triangle set (see Cutting the Strips, page 18). After the shapes are cut, refer to Design Possibilities (page 18) for ideas on how the shapes can be rotated for different looks. When you've determined the best look for each set of shapes, mark the center so you can piece them together appropriately.

2. Using 1 R triangle, 2 L flat pyramids, 4 M triangles, 1 D1 diamond, and 2 D2 triangles, arrange 1 wedge.

3. Sew 2 M triangles to the D1 diamond to make a triangle unit.

4. Sew 2 M triangles to the 2 L flat pyramids so they are a mirror image, as shown.

5. Sew the mirror-image units to the center triangle unit. Add the D2 triangles to the ends to make the lower unit.

6. Attach the R triangle to complete 1 wedge.

7. Make 6 identical wedges.

8. Arrange the wedges into a hexagon, with the repeat fabric at the center.

9. Sew the wedges into groups of 3 to make half-hexagons. Then sew the center seam to complete the block. Refer to Sewing and Pressing Options (page 32) if needed.

TIGERSTRIPE

Finished Tigerstripe block: 16½″ × 19″

The following yardage is for up to nine blocks, with all the blocks created from the same fabrics. If a variety of fabrics is desired throughout the nine blocks, read Using Multiple Fabrics per Shape (page 23) to figure yardage. Refer to General Information for Making Blocks (page 32) as needed.

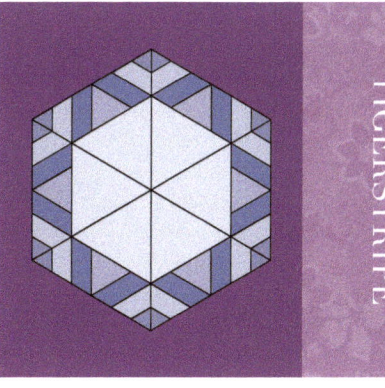

YARDAGE AND CUTTING

Cut the strips and corresponding shapes using the instructions on the pages noted in the table. Refer to Cutting the Strips (page 18) as needed.

FABRIC	YDG FOR 9 BLOCKS	STRIP QTY AND SIZE TO CUT FOR 9 BLOCKS	QTY, SHAPE, AND SIZE TO CUT FOR 9 BLOCKS	QTY OF SHAPE IN 1 BLOCK
REPEAT (R) (A set is 6 layers.)	Minimum of 24″ repeat or 4 yards	3 stacked strip sets 6¼″ × 20″	9 triangle sets 6¼″ (page 116)	1 set of 6
LIGHT 1 (L1)	¾ yard	12 strips 1⅞″ × WOF	108 strip-pieced triangles 3½″ (page 116)	12
MEDIUM (M)	½ yard	6 strips 2⅛″ × WOF		
LIGHT 2 (L2)	½ yard	3 strips 3½″ × WOF	54 triangles 3½″ (page 116)	6
DARK (D)	¾ yard	11 strips 1⅞″ × WOF	108 long diamonds 3¼″ (54 L and 54 R) (page 118)	12 (6 L and 6 R)

Piecing

Review General Information for Making Blocks (page 32). Seam allowances are ¼″ unless otherwise noted. Follow the arrows for pressing directions.

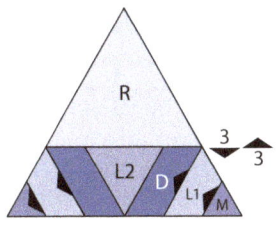

Tigerstripe wedge

1. Determine the best selection of a 6¼″ R triangle set (see Cutting the Strips, page 18). After the shapes are cut, refer to Design Possibilities (page 18) for ideas on how the shapes can be rotated for different looks. When you've determined the best look for each set of shapes, mark the center so you can piece them together appropriately.

2. Using 1 R triangle, 2 L1-M strip-pieced triangles, 1 L2 triangle, and 2 D long diamonds (1 left and 1 right), arrange 1 wedge.

3. Sew the D long diamonds to either side of the L2 triangle so they are a mirror image, as shown.

4. Sew the 2 L1-M strip-pieced triangles to the ends.

5. Attach the R triangle to complete 1 wedge.

6. Make 6 identical wedges.

7. Arrange the wedges into a hexagon, with the repeat fabric at the center.

8. Sew the wedges into groups of 3 to make half-hexagons. Then sew the center seam to complete the block. Refer to Sewing and Pressing Options (page 32) as needed.

WAVING FLAGS

Finished Waving Flags block: 16½˝ × 19˝

The following yardage is for up to nine blocks, with all the blocks created from the same fabrics. If a variety of fabrics is desired throughout the nine blocks, read Using Multiple Fabrics per Shape (page 23) to figure yardage. Refer to General Information for Making Blocks (page 32) as needed.

YARDAGE AND CUTTING

Cut the strips and corresponding shapes using the instructions on the pages noted in the table. Refer to Cutting the Strips (page 18) as needed.

FABRIC	YDG FOR 9 BLOCKS	STRIP QTY AND SIZE TO CUT FOR 9 BLOCKS	QTY, SHAPE, AND SIZE TO CUT FOR 9 BLOCKS	QTY OF SHAPE IN 1 BLOCK
REPEAT (R) (A set is 6 layers.)	Minimum of 18˝ repeat or 3 yards	3 stacked strip sets 3¼˝ × 20˝	9 diamond sets 3¼˝ (page 117)	1 set of 6
LIGHT (L)	⅞ yard	12 strips 1⅞˝ × WOF	108 strip-pieced triangles 3½˝ (page 116)	12
DARK 1 (D1)	½ yard	6 strips 2⅛˝ × WOF		
MEDIUM 1 (M1)	⅞ yard	6 strips 3½˝ × WOF	108 triangles 3½˝ (page 116)	12
MEDIUM 2 (M2)	½ yard	3 strips 3½˝ × WOF	54 triangles 3½˝ (page 116)	6
DARK 2 (D2)	¾ yard	11 strips 1⅞˝ × WOF	108 long diamonds 3¼˝ (54 L and 54 R) (page 118)	12 (6 L and 6 R)

Piecing

Review General Information for Making Blocks (page 32). Seam allowances are ¼˝ unless otherwise noted. Follow the arrows for pressing directions.

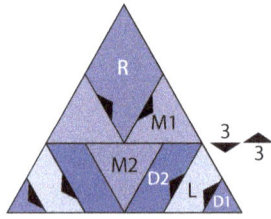

Waving Flags wedge

1. Determine the best selection of a 3¼˝ R diamond set (see Cutting the Strips, page 18). After the shapes are cut, refer to Design Possibilities (page 18) for ideas on how the shapes can be rotated for different looks. When you've determined the best look for each set of shapes, mark the center so you can piece them together appropriately.

2. Using 1 R diamond, 2 M1 triangles, 1 M2 triangle, 2 D2 long diamonds (1 left and 1 right), and 2 L-D1 strip-pieced triangles, arrange 1 wedge.

3. Sew the 2 M1 triangles to the non-center edges of the R diamond to make the upper unit.

4. Sew the 2 D2 long diamonds to either side of the M2 triangle. Add the 2 L-D1 strip-pieced triangles to the ends to make the lower unit.

5. Join the upper and lower units to complete 1 wedge.

6. Make 6 identical wedges.

7. Arrange the wedges into a hexagon, with the repeat fabric at the center.

8. Sew the wedges into groups of 3 to make half-hexagons. Then sew the center seam to complete the block. Refer to Sewing and Pressing Options (page 32) as needed.

WHIRLWIND

Finished Whirlwind block: 16½″ × 19″

The following yardage is for up to nine blocks, with all the blocks created from the same fabrics. If a variety of fabrics is desired throughout the nine blocks, read Using Multiple Fabrics per Shape (page 23) to figure yardage. Refer to General Information for Making Blocks (page 32) as needed.

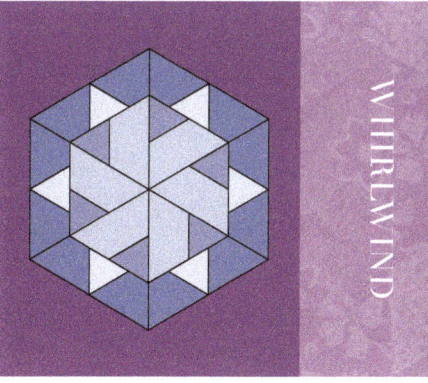

YARDAGE AND CUTTING

Cut the strips and corresponding shapes using the instructions on the pages noted in the table. Refer to Cutting the Strips (page 18) as needed.

FABRIC	YDG FOR 9 BLOCKS	STRIP QTY AND SIZE TO CUT FOR 9 BLOCKS	QTY, SHAPE, AND SIZE TO CUT FOR 9 BLOCKS	QTY OF SHAPE IN 1 BLOCK
REPEAT (R) (A set is 6 layers.)	Minimum of 18″ repeat or 3 yards	3 stacked strip sets 3¼″ × 20″	9 flat pyramid sets 6¼″ (page 121)	1 set of 6
LIGHT (L)	½ yard	3 strips 3½″ × WOF	54 triangles 3½″ (page 116)	6
MEDIUM (M)	½ yard	3 strips 3½″ × WOF	54 triangles 3½″ (page 116)	6
DARK (D)	1¼ yards	11 strips 3¼″ × WOF	108 flat pyramids 4⅞″ (page 121)	12

Piecing

Review General Information for Making Blocks (page 32). Seam allowances are ¼″ unless otherwise noted. Follow the arrows for pressing directions.

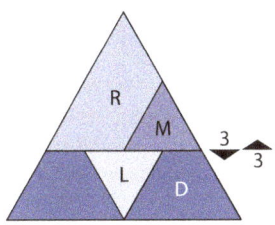

Whirlwind wedge

1. Determine the best selection of a 6¼″ R flat pyramid set (see Cutting the Strips, page 18). After the shapes are cut, refer to Design Possibilities (page 18) for ideas on how the shapes can be rotated for different looks. When you've determined the best look for each set of shapes, mark the center so you can piece them together appropriately.

2. Using 1 R flat pyramid, 1 L triangle, 1 M triangle, and 2 D flat pyramids, arrange 1 wedge.

3. Sew the M triangle to the R flat pyramid to make the upper unit.

4. Sew the 2 D flat pyramids on either side of the L triangle to make the lower unit.

5. Join the upper and lower units to complete 1 wedge. Make sure the desired end of the R flat pyramid is at the top of the wedge.

6. Make 6 identical wedges.

7. Arrange the wedges into a hexagon, with the repeat fabric at the center.

8. Sew the wedges into groups of 3 to make half-hexagons. Then sew the center seam to complete the block. Refer to Sewing and Pressing Options (page 32) as needed.

QUILT DESIGNS

Note

In each quilt design diagram, there are lines separating the blocks and setting triangles from the end pieces. At one end of the quilt is a simple finish, and the other end of the quilt has setting triangles involved in the design. Make your choice based on the resources available, including fabric, time, and patience.

Even though there is a variety of arrangements, each design is pieced in a similar manner. These basic instructions apply to all the quilt designs.

Arrange the blocks, setting triangles, and end pieces into the arrangement of the particular quilt design, and refer to the quilt assembly diagram for that design.

Flint by Joan Dawson, 67″ × 75″

Joan made seven strong blocks, but she just couldn't stop stacking these dainty, detailed flowers. These little bouquets became an inner border and the setting triangles. The corners are filled with butterfly appliqués. Outer border triangles all point in and add to a lacy, foamy look. Refer to the Flint block (page 43) and the Serendipity setting triangle (page 105).

72 STACK & CUT Hexagon Quilts

TWO-BLOCK DESIGN

As the simplest design, this is best made from leftover pieces. Add some setting triangles and a simple border to create a beautiful centerpiece or a wallhanging. See the quilt assembly diagram for where to place the setting triangles.

Finished size without borders: 16½″ × 38″ (simple ends) • 16½″ × 57″ (setting triangle ends)

YARDAGE AND CUTTING FOR FINISHING THE TOP

FABRIC	YDG FOR ENDS	STRIP QTY AND SIZE TO CUT FOR ENDS	QTY AND SHAPE TO CUT FOR ENDS
SIMPLE ENDS	⅜ yard	1 strip 5½″, subcut into 2 rectangles 5½″ × 9½″	2 L and 2 R triangle halves (page 115)
SETTING TRIANGLE ENDS	⅜ yard	1 strip 5½″, subcut into 2 rectangles 5½″ × 9½″	2 L and 2 R triangle halves (page 115)

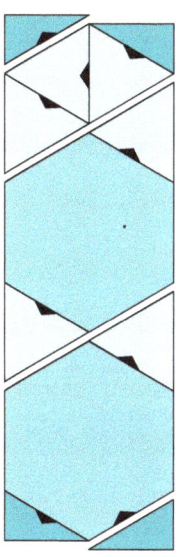

Two-block quilt assembly

A table runner in springlike colors—blue sky, fresh green shoots, yellow buttercups, and still a touch of ice in shady corners. Nature and quilters can make a lot out of a little. Refer to the Dutch Star block (page 41) and the Serendipity setting triangle (page 105).

Dutch Star Leftovers by Kate McIntyre, 22″ × 51″

Quilt Designs

THREE-BLOCK DESIGN

Here are two very different designs for three blocks. The first is an extension of the two-block table runner/wallhanging. The second puts the blocks in a round shape with setting triangles and units from the block designs. Use the three-block quilt assembly diagrams (below and next page) to sew the pieces together. For binding these different angles, refer to Binding Other Angles (page 123).

Finished size without borders: 16½″ × 57″ (simple ends) • 16½″ × 76″ (pieced ends)
Finished size with borders: 38½″ × 44½″

YARDAGE AND CUTTING FOR FINISHING THE TOP

FABRIC	YDG FOR ENDS	STRIP QTY AND SIZE TO CUT FOR ENDS	QTY AND SHAPE TO CUT FOR ENDS
SIMPLE ENDS	⅜ yard	1 strip 5½″, subcut into 2 rectangles 5½″ × 9½″	2 L and 2 R triangle halves (page 115)
SETTING TRIANGLE ENDS	⅜ yard	1 strip 5½″, subcut into 2 rectangles 5½″ × 9½″	2 L and 2 R triangle halves (page 115)

Butterflies in My Garden by Diane Gilbreath, 24½″ × 65″

Bright colors make a pretty table runner with just three blocks. The repeat fabric is used as the border and still surprises with the stars that result from stacking. Diana appliquéd four butterflies from the repeat fabric to add a little more charm to the design. Refer to the Starry Path block (page 65) and the Serendipity setting triangle (page 105). For complete project instructions, see Three-Block Table Runner (page 24).

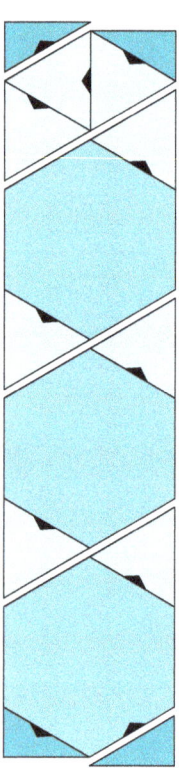

Three-block quilt assembly 1 (in a line)

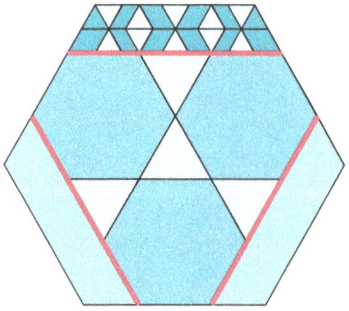

Three-block design 2 (in the round)

74 STACK & CUT Hexagon Quilts

YARDAGE AND CUTTING FOR FINISHING THE TOP

FABRIC	YDG FOR ENDS	STRIP QTY AND SIZE TO CUT FOR ENDS	QTY AND SHAPE TO CUT FOR ENDS
SIMPLE ENDS	¾ yard	3 strips 6″	3 rectangles 6″ × 29″
PIECED ENDS	⅜ yard of light	2 strips 3½″	30 triangles 3½″ (page 116)
	½ yard of dark	3 strips 3¼″	30 diamonds 3¼″ (page 117)
		1 strip 3½″	6 triangles 3½″ (page 116)

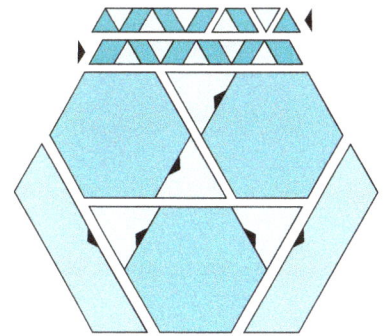

Three-block quilt assembly 2 (in the round)

Park Place
by Marci Baker,
38½″ × 44½″

Detail of redwork in *Park Place*

This is a beautiful interpretation of redwork. What wonderful designs a repeat fabric creates with this red-and-white floral print! A simple combination of red diamonds and white triangles was Marci's choice for the setting triangles—resulting in light, medium, and dark diamonds that begin to have a three-dimensional look. Refer to the Park Place block (page 52) and the Chestnut setting triangle (page 103).

Quilt Designs

FOUR-BLOCK DESIGN

The diamond shape created with four blocks is intriguing. With the blocks floating on the background fabric, the designs stand out. The piecing is easy with this structure. Use the four-block quilt assembly diagram (below) to sew your blocks together for a simple yet elegant project.

Finished size without borders: 38″ × 49½″

YARDAGE AND CUTTING FOR FINISHING THE TOP

FABRIC	YDG FOR ENDS	STRIP QTY AND SIZE TO CUT FOR ENDS	QTY AND SHAPE TO CUT FOR ENDS
SIMPLE ENDS	1 yard	2 strips 15″, subcut into 2 rectangles 15″ × 26″	2 L and 2 R triangle halves (page 115)
SETTING TRIANGLE ENDS	⅝ yard	2 strips 5½″, subcut into 6 rectangles 5½″ × 9½″	6 L and 6 R triangle halves (page 115)

Four-block quilt assembly

Many Winds by Janice Jamison, 50″ × 61″

Little Garden by Janet Blazekovich, 50″ × 59″

The high contrast background—much darker than the stars and hexagons—allows the shapes to look like jewels created by a master craftsman. All the precise details add to the idea of perfection. A smaller number of blocks makes it easier to see every part of the design. Refer to the Whirlwind block (page 71) and the Serendipity setting triangle (page 105).

Beautiful contrast is created with this complementary color scheme of deep sea blue, coral, and salmon. If you look closely, sand dollars, starfish, and sea urchins appear. Janet had extra stacked repeat fabric, so she decided to fill in the corners with simple diamond and triangle designs. Refer to the Little Garden block (page 47) and the Serendipity (page 105) and Shamrock (page 106) setting triangles.

FIVE-BLOCK DESIGN

In this quilt design, notice that the blocks are turned sideways so the flat sides are at the top and bottom. This gives a different proportion to the quilt, enabling Sara to get a nice throw-size quilt using only five blocks and a nice-size border (see *Tigerstripe*, below left). Use the five-block quilt assembly diagram (below) to see where to place the setting triangles and how to sew it together.

Finished size without borders: 38″ × 49½″

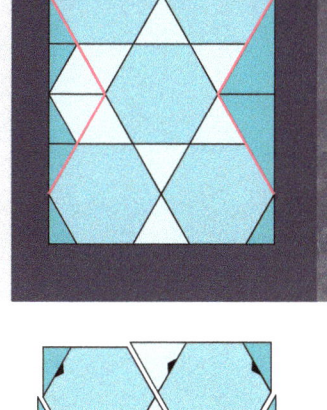

YARDAGE AND CUTTING FOR FINISHING THE TOP

FABRIC	YDG FOR ENDS	STRIP QTY AND SIZE TO CUT FOR ENDS	QTY AND SHAPE TO CUT FOR ENDS
SIMPLE ENDS	¾ yard	1 strip 10¼″, subcut into 2 rectangles 10¼″ × 17¾″	2 L and 2 R triangle halves (page 115)
		1 strip 5½″, subcut into 2 rectangles 5½″ × 9½″	2 L and 2 R triangle halves (page 115)
SETTING TRI-ANGLE ENDS	⅝ yard	2 strips 5½″, subcut into 6 rectangles 5½″ × 9½″	6 L and 6 R triangle halves (page 115)

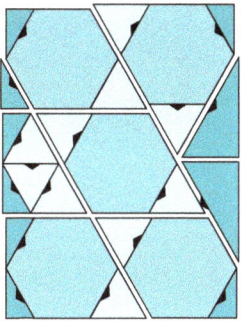

Five-block quilt assembly

Tigerstripe by Sara Nephew, quilted by Pam Cope, 50¼″ × 65¾″. Inset: Repeat fabric for *Tigerstripe*.

A garage sale fabric is the inspiration for a fun quilt. This pet deer fabric makes pretty and unusual stars when it's cut up. There was only enough for five large blocks, so Sara chose not to use the small stacked hexagons in the setting triangles, instead filling the connecting spaces with assorted pastel colors. The edges and corners are squared off with a light purple, and the Double Diamond border (page 111) completes the quilt. Refer to the Tigerstripe block (page 69) and the Shamrock setting triangle (page 106).

Frozen by Marci Baker, 36½″ × 45½″.

Beginning with a curvy, light floral design, the resulting flower and windmill designs evoke a bright, sunny spring day with a light, cool breeze. They appear to float above the background field of flowers, displaying the beauty of each and every one. Refer to the Frozen block (page 44) and the Serendipity setting triangle (page 105).

Quilt Designs 77

Six-block design (shifted columns)

SIX-BLOCK DESIGN

There are few options for making the six-block design. But to make the layout more proportional for a lap quilt, Laurie Biundo used a few setting triangles at the top or bottom of the column and shifted the center column down in *Park Place* (variation) (below). The hexagons appear around the blocks rather than stars, though Laurie did extend some stars into the border to highlight a few.

Follow the six-block quilt assembly diagram (below) for piecing the blocks and setting triangles together with the shifted column. For fun, we have added an illustration of what it would look like if it was not shifted.

Finished size (shifted columns): 44½″ × 49½″

Finished size (not shifted columns): 47½″ × 49½″

YARDAGE AND CUTTING FOR FINISHING THE TOP

FABRIC	YDG FOR ENDS	STRIP QTY AND SIZE TO CUT FOR ENDS	QTY AND SHAPE TO CUT FOR ENDS
Simple ends (for quilt design that is not shifted)	¾ yard	1 strip 10¼″, subcut into 2 rectangles 10¼″ × 17¾″	2 L and 2 R triangle halves (page 115)
		1 strip 5½″, subcut into 2 rectangles 5½″ × 9½″	2 L and 2 R triangle halves (page 115)
SETTING TRIANGLE ENDS	⅝ yard	2 strips 5½″, subcut into 6 rectangles 5½″ × 9½″	6 L and 6 R triangle halves (page 115)

Six-block quilt assembly (not shifted)

Six-block quilt assembly (shifted columns)

Park Place (variation) by Laurie Biundo, 42½″ × 54″

Laurie created a new layout for the setting triangles at the top and bottom of the quilt by shifting the columns of blocks and cleverly adding triangles in the left and right borders to complete the smaller stars. These blocks offer a wonderful opportunity to be creative with appliqué, embroidery, or even beading. Refer to the Park Place block (page 52) and the Smile setting triangle (page 107).

SEVEN-BLOCK DESIGN

The design with seven blocks and hexagons is a very pleasing structure. Like a grandmother's flower garden, one hexagon is central and the others surround it in a complete ring. With the repeat-fabric design, the structure is a mandala in its own right, enabling designs with a strong circular look.

Finished size without borders: 49½″ × 57″

YARDAGE AND CUTTING FOR FINISHING THE TOP

FABRIC	YDG FOR ENDS	STRIP QTY AND SIZE TO CUT FOR ENDS	QTY AND SHAPE TO CUT FOR ENDS
SIMPLE ENDS	1 yard	2 strips 15″, subcut into 2 rectangles 15″ × 26″	2 L and 2 R triangle halves (page 115)
SETTING TRIANGLE ENDS	⅝ yard	2 strips 5½″, subcut into 6 rectangles 5½″ × 9½″	6 L and 6 R triangle halves (page 115)

Seven-block quilt assembly

Pink Power by Kate McIntyre, 78″ × 85½″. Inset: Repeat fabric for *Pink Power*.

Protect and Serve by Linda Rose DeGaeta, 57″ × 73½″

Kate McIntyre and Benita Cole like to challenge each other to use the same fabric in their two different quilts (see *Porthole*, page 97, for Benita's design). Kate made a large quilt from just seven blocks with borders and corner squares—very pretty and feminine. Using some dark colors brings out and emphasizes the block design, while the gold color adds a mellow touch. Refer to the Dutch Star block (page 41) and the Serendipity setting triangle (page 105).

This quilt demonstrates an innovative use of special figured prints in a stacked repeat. Flags, police officers, fire trucks, helicopters, police cars, and more definitely establish the theme. A new shape of setting triangles holds some of the larger pictures, which are then surrounded with strong star points: part of the design that adds emphasis. Refer to the Flashdance block (page 42) and the Starburst setting triangle (page 108).

Masquerade by Linda Rose DeGaeta, 56″ × 60½″

This is a much larger star, designed with four rows of graph-paper triangles instead of three. Linda used fabric that looks like metallic lines sewn onto dark fabric with lots of decorative detail, creating a lacy filigree effect. Shaded purple triangles glow among the dark corners, while fabric like gold lace picks up an echo of the center. Linda tops it all off with her special border, a 60° design inspired by the book *French Braid Quilts* by Jane Hardy Miller with Arlene Netten (by C&T Publishing). This block is a combination of the Badge block (page 34) and the Sonata block (page 63) for an even larger design. If you like a challenge, see if you can put the pieces together.

Repeat fabric for *The Buzz*

The Buzz by Linda Rose DeGaeta, 57½″ × 62″

Linda enjoyed making *Masquerade* (above) so much she felt compelled to make a second one. She experimented with values and color, trying something completely different. Notice how the strong designs of the repeat fabric create a swirl of motion. The elements created by the print are more prominent than in her first version because of the high contrast in the yellow, black, and white fabric.

Galaxy of Stars by Janice Jamison, 63″ × 65″

Gold stars on a textured bronze background make the whole quilt look like a Medal of Honor. The repeat fabric in hexagons of turquoise, purple, white, and black look like flashing diamonds, even though the shapes and lines created by stacking the fabrics are often curved—a surprise in every quilt! Refer to the Patriot block (page 53) and the Darling setting triangle (page 104).

Poinsettia by Joan Dawson, 64″ × 71″. Inset: Repeat fabric for *Poinsettia*.

Photos by Randy Pfizenmeier

The shapes of this block echo the Christmas plant, the poinsettia, so Joan chose red and green, a complementary color scheme. These shapes and colors explode like fireworks—Christmas style! Refer to the Poinsettia block (page 54) and the Darling (page 104) and Serendipity (page 105) setting triangles.

Repeat fabric for *Prickly Pear*

Prickly Pear by Becky Dietz and Marci Baker, 53″ × 70″

All the sharp triangle points around the edge of each block make this pattern prickly. The turquoise, chartreuse, and blue are quite a sharp color combination, too. The black triangles and white diamonds of the setting triangles create a strong design to hold it all together, and the white diamonds circle between the blocks. Refer to the Prickly Pear block (page 56) and the Chestnut setting triangle (page 103).

Quilt Designs

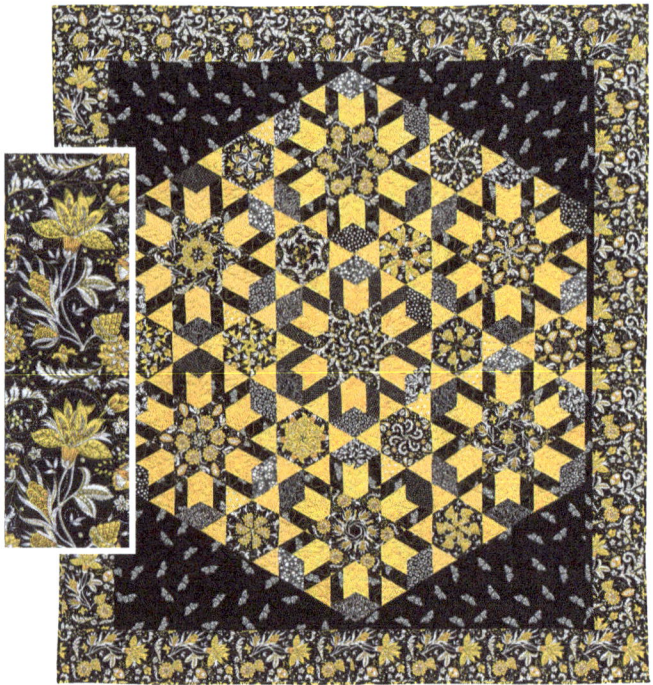

Ringstone by Joan Dawson, 62″ × 69½″. Inset: Repeat fabric for *Ringstone*.

Careful examination reveals that this one busy fabric makes the border and all the busy fabrics in the stacked stars and hexagons of the quilt. For the rest, Joan used black-and-white or gray-and-white prints, combined with a few yellow fabrics. This, by the way, is the same fabric used in *The Buzz* (page 80). Refer to the Ringstone block (page 57) and the Serendipity setting triangle (page 105).

Ringstone Variation by Joan Dawson, 61″ × 68″. Inset: Repeat fabric for *Ringstone Variation*.

Joan loves Serendipity blocks so much that she started designing her own. After she made the original *Ringstone* quilt (at left), she wondered what would happen if she flipped the position of the light and dark long diamonds. Add a different fabric, and you realize these quilt variations are endless.

Shimmer by Pamela Seaberg, 56″ × 61″

An interesting layout of simple blocks and setting triangles is transformed by a floral print to take your breath away. Pamela added to the success with appliquéd flowers in the corners. (Are those orchids?) Then a pretty inner border of tiny triangles adds a touch of lace to the bouquet. This is a combination of the Susan block (page 67), the centers of the Susan block, and the Serendipity setting triangle (page 105).

Two-Sided Serendipity Sampler by Virginia L. Anderson, 56″ × 63″

Back of *Two-Sided Serendipity Sampler* by Virginia L. Anderson

Photos by Randy Pfizenmeier

Virginia chose blocks she liked and worked them out with light print fabrics that have a thirties flavor (though all are modern fabrics). She carried out that theme in the setting triangles, as well: Dark brown and stronger red and blue accents emphasize the structure of the overall design. Colorful triangles and zigzag strips make a great border, expanding beyond the center structure like rays. The barbershop striped binding is the perfect edge finish to pick up the colors in the quilt. Virginia is in control of every element of this quilt. She made more blocks and put the extras on the back. Refer to the Serendipity setting triangle (page 105) and the Zigzag border (page 114).

Owls Have Shy Eyes by Kate McIntyre, 83½″ × 97″

Little triangles and white diamonds make this quilt sparkle, and an original layout makes an almost-smooth circle. Kate eliminated the in-between setting triangles by sharing parts from each block with the adjacent blocks. With careful planning, you can do all kinds of clever things. Refer to the Shy Eyes block (page 62) and the Chestnut setting triangle (page 103).

Quilt Designs

Jungle Fever by Cindy Glancy, 58″ × 65″. Inset: Repeat fabric for *Jungle Fever*.

High contrast and wonderfully graphic, the hot colors in this design are ideal with the tropical repeat fabric of parrots, flowers, and lots of greenery. Because of cutting choices, not much green shows—it's nighttime in the jungle. Cindy created a round mandala of amazing shapes and colors. There is a lot to look at here! Refer to the Sonata block (page 63) and the Serendipity setting triangle (page 105).

A Child's Christmas by Linda Rose DeGaeta, quilted by Janice Jameson, 62″ × 71½″

Fairies dance on a summer night. (And you thought those were fireflies!) Is that a yellow moon beginning to show through the trees? Wonderful dreams are ahead for whoever sleeps under this quilt. Purple and yellow are complementary colors, made richer by red, black, and green accents. Refer to the Stained Glass block (page 64) and the Starburst setting triangle (page 108).

Photos by Randy Pfizenmeier

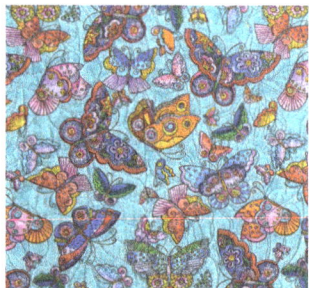

Repeat fabric for *Waving Flags*.

Waving Flags by Kathie Kryla, 61″ × 69″

Pale pink and blue can be hard to work with, but Kathie seems to have the colors well under control. An assortment of pinks picks up the colors in the repeat fabric, and a variety of purples and blues supplies a rich effect in the quilt colors. Kathy used seven large blocks and created many more small stacked hexagons. They are everywhere in the border and throughout the quilt. Refer to the Waving Flags block (page 70), the Serendipity setting triangle (page 105), and the Bunting border (page 110).

Cubes in My Garden by Janice Jameson, 64″ × 70″

This looks like just a simple design until you look closer and see the fine details in the hexagons throughout the quilt. This strong design is like looking through a microscope at all the star-like diatoms floating in the ocean. Janice also put some hollow cubes into a few of the setting triangles, perhaps influenced by her friend, Linda Rose DeGaeta. Refer to the Little Garden block (page 47). While this quilt uses the seven-block setting, look closely and you'll see four half-blocks used to finish the quilt.

Mood Indigo by Linda Rose DeGaeta, quilted by Janice Jameson, 61½″ × 69″

Beautiful border prints create marvelous and changing combinations as they show up in the blocks and setting triangles. Half-blocks are another graceful way to fill in the corners. This builds on the seven-block layout for a wider quilt. Refer to the Sailor's Dream block (page 60) and the Serendipity (page 105) and Starburst (page 108) setting triangles.

Quilt Designs

EIGHT-BLOCK DESIGN

With the seven-block design, the rows had two, three, and two blocks in them consecutively. If there is an extra block, the order is then three, two, and three blocks. This results in a quilt of the same size while displaying an additional intriguing design.

Finished size without borders: 49½″ × 57″

YARDAGE AND CUTTING FOR FINISHING THE TOP

FABRIC	YDG FOR ENDS	STRIP QTY AND SIZE TO CUT FOR ENDS	QTY AND SHAPE TO CUT FOR ENDS
SIMPLE ENDS	¾ yard	1 strip 10¼″, subcut into 2 rectangles 10¼″ × 17¾″	2 L and 2 R triangle halves (page 115)
		1 strip 5½″, subcut into 2 rectangles 5½″ × 9½″	2 L and 2 R triangle halves (page 115)
SETTING TRIANGLE ENDS	⅝ yard	2 strips 5½″, subcut into 6 rectangles 5½″ × 9½″	6 L and 6 R triangle halves (page 115)

Eight-block quilt assembly

Persian Carpet from Singapore by Romona Melnick, 60″ × 67½″

Photo by Randy Pfizenmeier

With a large center and a plain outer border, this block seems almost too simple … until Ramona chose to put very complicated fabric into it. The fabric patterns are finely detailed and textured, evoking a sari made of embroidered silk or an etching engraved into bronze. Look closely to see all the different designs. Refer to the Little Garden block (page 47) and the Serendipity setting triangle (page 105).

See *Knotted Cord* (page 27) for another example of an eight-block quilt design.

NINE-BLOCK DESIGN

This is the most common quilt design used throughout the book. With this quantity of blocks, the quilt is closer to a traditional bed-size piece. Adding borders makes it fit a full- or queen-size bed.

Finished size without borders: 49½″ × 66½″

YARDAGE AND CUTTING FOR FINISHING THE TOP

FABRIC	YDG FOR ENDS	STRIP QTY AND SIZE TO CUT FOR ENDS	QTY AND SHAPE TO CUT FOR ENDS
SIMPLE ENDS	¾ yard	1 strip 10¼″, subcut into 2 rectangles 10¼″ × 17¾″	2 L and 2 R triangle halves (page 115)
		1 strip 5½″, subcut into 2 rectangles 5½″ × 9½″	2 L and 2 R triangle halves (page 115)
SETTING TRI-ANGLE ENDS	⅝ yard	2 strips 5½″, subcut into 6 rectangles 5½″ × 9½″	6 L and 6 R triangle halves (page 115)

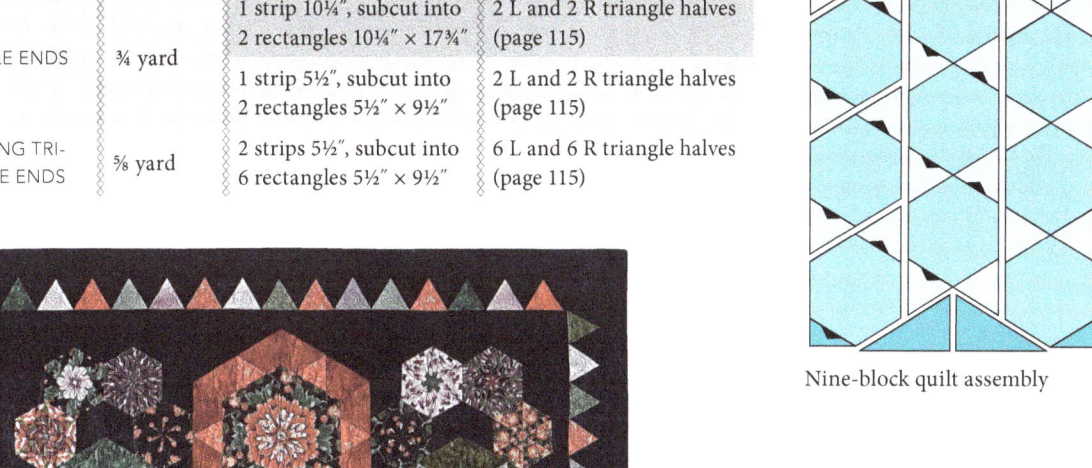

Nine-block quilt assembly

Badge by Pamela Seaberg, 62″ × 79″

Photo by Randy Pfizenmeier

Pamela chose a fabric that cut up into a surprising assortment of colors and designs—a great choice. Some blocks feature the star, and others create a ring of color around the center of the star. Add simple triangles as a decorative border so the different triangle colors pick up and emphasize different blocks and setting units. Refer to the Badge block (page 34) and the Serendipity setting triangle (page 105).

Bezel by Cindy Fredrick, 63½˝ × 80½˝

A soft pale yellow around the outside corners of every block adds movement and contrast that really makes this quilt design work. Darkly glowing bouquets fill the rest of the quilt—a strong statement. Refer to the Bezel block (page 35) and the Serendipity setting triangle (page 105).

Button by Janet Blazekovich, 57˝ × 74½˝. Inset: Repeat fabric for *Button*.

What a surprising and beautiful combination of colors and shapes! The multicolor repeat fabric is cooled and balanced by two shades of blue, plus black. This creates separate shapes that could be microscopic creatures or jewels from a master craftsman. Janet added smaller design hexagons to create a border with more interesting detail. Refer to the Button block (page 37) and the Serendipity setting triangle (page 105).

Dainty by Kathy Syring, 56½˝ × 72˝

Dark purple and light creamy yellow create high contrast and strong structure. At the same time, fabric details produce multiple shades and tints of colors in between purple and yellow. There are practically unlimited designs to look at! Refer to the Dainty block (page 39) and the Serendipity setting triangle (page 105).

Dewdrops by Alicia B. Sanchez, 61½" × 79"

White hexagons in the setting triangles are drops of dew-like glowing pearls. What an original approach, inspired by the block name! The dark and light blocks create a strong pattern with a flavor of the Southwest. Alicia outdid herself, scattering various tiny dewdrops reflecting images of the larger blocks on two corners of the quilt. Refer to the Dew block (page 40) and the Smile setting triangle (page 107).

Could've Should've by Elaine Muzichuk, 63" × 80"

Elaine used her repeat fabric as a border, so it's fascinating to look at the original fabric and then find it in the stars and setting triangles with a surprising new look. Off-white added to the stars emphasizes the warm colors and the structure of the design. Narrow inner borders, especially the red, are great accents. Refer to the Magic block (page 48) and the Serendipity setting triangle (page 105).

Moonglow by Elaine Muzichuk, 67" × 83½"

Elaine picked bright, cheery colors for her quilt. The star points make a strong pattern across the quilt, and the hot orange batik creates an aura around the big hexagons. Moonglow indeed! Refer to the Moonglow block (page 50) and the Serendipity setting triangle (page 105).

Repeat fabric for *Starstruck*

Starstruck by Janet Blazekovich, 62½″ × 81″
Inset:

Janet likes a lot of color; it's easy to see. This time her quilt has diagonal rows that are outlined in blue, orange, and green. The repeat fabric in the large blocks and small hexagons has those colors and many more to please the eye. A light blue as a background and a wide blue border finishes the design. Refer to the Moonglow block (page 50) and the Serendipity setting triangle (page 105).

Photo by Randy Pfizenmeier

Ornament by Pamela York, 66½″ × 83½″

Soft teal blue and a caramel-color brown are an unusual, antique-looking color combination. Pamela emphasized the aged look by adding a border fabric that seems to look like parchment or papyrus. Soft white or unbleached muslin adds some strong contrast. Refer to the Ornament block (page 51) and the Serendipity setting triangle (page 105).

Ripples by Sara Nephew, quilted by Judy Irish, 59½" × 76½"

Inspired by fabrics found at garage sales—a narrow leafy green and yellow stripe, plus a rich floral print—Sara began digging in her stash for more checks and stripes in peach, pink, and light blue. A few darker colors show the structure of the star blocks and setting triangles. A printed blue border makes a cooler finish. Refer to the Ripples block (page 58) and the Serendipity setting triangle (page 105).

Photo by Randy Pfizenmeier

Rose Window by Martha Ethridge, 60" × 77"

Mint and raspberries make a luscious dish with delicate flowers scattered over all. Looks good enough to eat! A strong dark border holds all the movement of the fabric designs inside. Refer to the Rose Window block (page 59) and the Serendipity setting triangle (page 105).

Quilt Designs 91

Sunshine & Shadow by Linda Rose DeGaeta, quilted by Janice Jameson, 71½″ × 88½″

Linda made a few changes to the Sailor's Dream block (page 60) and had a new design to sew. Perhaps she used more than one repeat fabric in this quilt—it's easy to want to try all the fabrics in your stash when you're having fun! This can result in a wide variety of blocks. Then you arrange the blocks, piling them one upon another and climbing into the sky. A fancy border fences in the design. Refer to the Sailor's Star block (page 61) and the Starburst setting triangle (page 108). For the border, Linda was inspired by Jane Hardy Miller's book *French Braid Quilts* (by C&T Publishing).

Starstruck by Sara Nephew, quilted by Judy Irish, 57½″ × 74½″

A variety of snowflakes were scattered over blue fabric. The laciness of the flakes is emphasized by the rich detail of an architectural-inspired print. The border is also full of details, which carries out the textured feeling of the whole quilt. Refer to the Starstruck block (page 66) and the Serendipity setting triangle (page 105).

Photos by Randy Pfizenmeier

Repeat fabric for *Double, Double, Toil and Trouble*

Double, Double, Toil and Trouble by Katie Kennedy, 69″ × 86″

This looks like a Mardi Gras quilt—time for partying, dancing, parades, music, and costumes! Wonderful shapes were created by stacking this fabric. The medium blue background cools everything down a little and adds some calm. So does the narrow green border, and all is held together by black. The black also picks up many of the details in the fireworks. Refer to the Susan block (page 67) and the Serendipity setting triangle (page 105).

Photos by Randy Pfizenmeier

Flight of Dragons by Linda Rose DeGaeta, 69½″ × 85½″

Linda used unusual theme fabric as the repeat for this quilt. When you look closely, you see knights who are ready to fight dragons. The dragons are there, too! Unusual shapes are created, and rich designs result. This quilt could be a castle wallhanging. Some of the blocks even look like cathedral stained glass windows. Note the extra half-blocks used to finish the quilt setting, all topped off by Linda's fabulous border inspired by Jane Hardy Miller's *French Braid Quilts* (by C&T Publishing). Refer to the Ticktock block (page 68) and the Serendipity (page 105) and Smile (page 107) setting triangles.

Quilt Designs

TEN-BLOCK DESIGN

Finished size without borders: 49½" × 76"

By adding one block in the center column of the nine-block design, the quilt is more proportional for traditional bed sizes. Having one more block design on the quilt brings even more intrigue to the overall design.

YARDAGE AND CUTTING FOR FINISHING THE TOP

FABRIC	YDG FOR ENDS	STRIP QTY AND SIZE TO CUT FOR ENDS	QTY AND SHAPE TO CUT FOR ENDS
SIMPLE ENDS	1 yard	2 strips 15", subcut into 2 rectangles 15" × 26"	2 L and 2 R triangle halves (page 115)
SETTING TRIANGLE ENDS	⅝ yard	2 strips 5½", subcut into 6 rectangles 5½" × 9½"	6 L and 6 R triangle halves (page 115)

Ten-block quilt assembly

Scrap Star by Sara Nephew, quilted by Judy Irish, 51" × 53½"

Repeat fabric for *Scrap Star*

After using the pet deer fabric (at right) in *Tigerstripe* (page 77), Sara had more small stacked hexagons left over. With a little careful cutting, she eked out fourteen altogether. The Crystal block is a simple two-unit design that makes it easy to use leftover fabrics in. Adding the Rickrack border (page 112) is a special touch. Refer to the Crystal block (page 38).

Scarlet Knight by Linda Rose DeGaeta, quilted by Janice Jameson, 62″ × 74½″

Linda just couldn't stop making blocks, stars, and hexagons. By the time she was finished, she had enough parts for two quilts. This quilt has a plain border instead of a pieced one. The quilt design emphasizes tiny light diamonds and triangles that put a sparkly pattern over the surface of the quilt, a dancing movement that adds life to the whole piece. Notice that the borders are wider on the sides than on the top and bottom. This is a great way to make a quilt design fit the purpose of the project. Refer to the Ticktock block (page 68) and the Darling (page 104) and Serendipity (page 105) setting triangles.

Quilt Designs

ELEVEN-BLOCK DESIGN

Finished size without borders: 49½″ × 76″

The largest design in this book, the eleven-block design, has longer columns on the outside and shorter columns on the inside. What an opportunity to show off your large-scale print fabrics!

YARDAGE AND CUTTING FOR FINISHING THE TOP

FABRIC	YDG FOR ENDS	STRIP QTY AND SIZE TO CUT FOR ENDS	QTY AND SHAPE TO CUT FOR ENDS
SIMPLE ENDS	¾ yard	1 strip 10¼″, subcut into 2 rectangles 10¼″ × 17¾″	2 L and 2 R triangle halves (page 115)
		1 strip 5½″, subcut into 2 rectangles 5½″ × 9½″	2 L and 2 R triangle halves (page 115)
SETTING TRIANGLE ENDS	⅝ yard	2 strips 5½″, subcut into 6 rectangles 5½″ × 9½″	6 L and 6 R triangle halves (page 115)

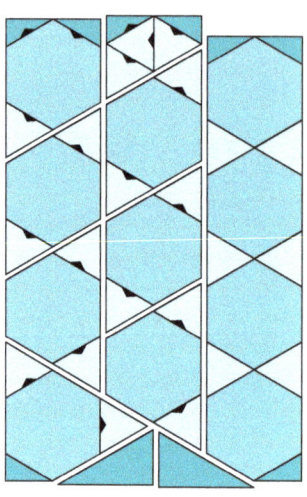

Eleven-block quilt assembly

Repeat fabric for *Porthole*

Porthole by Benita Cole, 65½″ × 91½″

Benita used the same fabric as Kate McIntyre did in *Pink Power* (page 79), but the final effect is quite different. This is a simple pattern, with the outside row just a strip of fabric. The quilt has just one plain border (if you don't count the sneaky thin strip of pink inside that border). So it's very simple, but there's a lot to look at. The featured print creates many different stars and hexagons. Refer to the Porthole block (page 55) and the Serendipity setting triangle (page 105).

OTHER QUILT DESIGNS
BLOCKS-ONLY SETTINGS

For a different effect, the blocks can be placed next to each other with no setting triangles. With smaller easily pieced blocks, this is a simple way to start and can be quite effective. Look at *Lamp* and *Lamp Variation* (page 100). When placed next to each other, the blocks start to create secondary patterns as seen in *Bold Star* (page 99). For these quilt designs, the blocks are left as half-blocks. They are positioned as desired, and the half-blocks are sewn together in rows; then the rows come together to finish the overall quilt.

YARDAGE AND CUTTING FOR FINISHING THE TOP

FABRIC	YDG FOR ENDS	STRIP QTY AND SIZE TO CUT FOR ENDS	QTY AND SHAPE TO CUT FOR ENDS
SMALL BLOCK DESIGN (11″ × 12¾″)	¼ yard	1 strip 3⅞″, subcut into 2–5 rectangles 3⅞″ × 6¾″	Up to 10 total L or R triangle halves (page 115)
	+ ⅛ yard	For each additional 5 rectangles needed	
LARGE BLOCK DESIGN (16½″ × 19″)	⅜ yard	1 strip 5½″, subcut into 4 rectangles 5½″ × 9½″	Up to 8 total L or R triangle halves (page 115)
	+ ¼ yard	For each additional 4 rectangles needed	

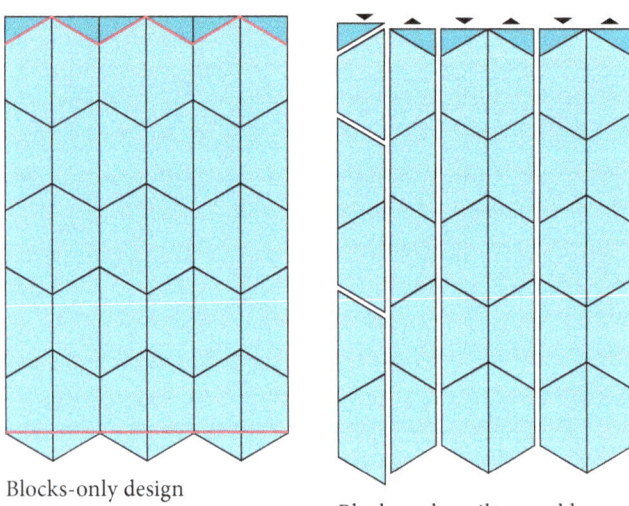

Blocks-only design

Blocks-only quilt assembly

This form can have many possibilities for the ends, so use the one that matches closest to your design. Use the yardage and cutting for the end pieces accordingly.

Bold Star by Marci Baker, 28½″ × 40½″

What a dramatic and bold effect! Using only four blocks and no setting triangles, this table topper shows how a secondary design can be achieved. The yellow accent triangles radiate for a dazzling display. Refer to the Bold Star block (page 36).

Repeat fabric for *Bold Star*.

Quilt Designs

Lamp by Laurie Biundo, 38½″ × 41½″

A very simple block, pieced in a striking and modern way. One block has reversed values and especially catches the eye. This creative approach brings up ideas about what else a person could do with the block. Appliqué could completely change this. And what about embroidery or fancy machine quilting? Refer to the Lamp block (page 46).

Lamp Variation by Marci Baker, 39″ × 53″

Having made many three-dimensional designs, Marci couldn't resist using that technique here. Focus on the Y-shape and there appears to be buildings that the repeat designs are sitting among; however, look at the repeat designs and rooms appear, with the repeat shapes resting in the corner (though nothing is resting with these bright, cheery colors!). This is a simple design with an intriguing twist.

SMALLER BLOCK SETTINGS

Using smaller blocks opens up the opportunity for different settings, as seen in the examples below.

Photo by Randy Pfizenmeier

A Star is Born by Linda Rose DeGaeta, 51″ × 63″

Linda had fun here adding some three-dimensional shapes to the design. In fact, she added other elements, too. An experienced quilter can enjoy many techniques and combine them to make something that is all his or hers. Here, stacked repeats and pieced radiating stars like a Texas Star are done at a 60° angle, and even an appliquéd butterfly is added. Confident designing is very satisfying.

Repeat fabric for *Mix & Match* (hexagonal blocks)

Repeat fabric for *Mix & Match* (star blocks)

Mix & Match by Janet Blazekovich, 55″ × 68″

There are two different designs of blocks in this quilt. Can you tell the star blocks from those made with six simple wedges? Janet used two different stacked fabrics and created a wonderfully colored combination. She added a cool-blue background fabric to balance out the other colors. Refer to the Mix & Match block (page 49).

Quilt Designs   101

SETTING TRIANGLE DESIGNS

Setting triangles bring the blocks together. A number of the quilts in this book use the stacked repeat fabric to make the Serendipity setting triangle (page 105). However, other fabrics can be used when there is not enough repeat fabric or to bring in another design element or coloration.

Remember that the repeat fabric listed in each block's yardage and cutting table includes enough fabric for 9 blocks and 24 sets of 3½″ triangles to be used as setting triangles, if desired.

The following charts include yardage and cutting for 24 setting triangles.

SINGLE TRIANGLE

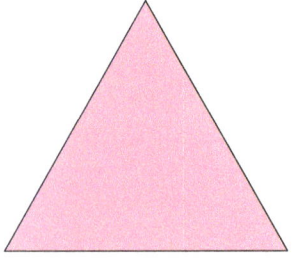

A simple single triangle can be used effectively, as shown in *Scrap Star* (page 94), *Mix & Match* (page 101), *A Star is Born* (page 101), and the back side of *Two-Sided Serendipity Sampler* (page 83). The first three blocks use 6¼″ (cut) triangles, and the last one uses a 9″ (cut) setting triangle. These are basically the same size as the wedge of the block design.

CHESTNUT

Two simple shapes make this intriguing design. With only three triangles and three diamonds, a chain around the blocks can be created. Or it can be an extension of the block to create six-pointed stars. For examples, see *Knotted Cord* (page 27), *Park Place* (page 75), *Prickly Pear* (page 81), and *Owls Have Shy Eyes* (page 83).

Finished Chestnut setting triangle: 8¼″

YARDAGE AND CUTTING

Cut the strips and corresponding shapes using the instructions on the pages noted in the table. Refer to Figuring Yardage for Setting Triangles (page 30) for other quantities.

FABRIC	WW	STRIP QTY AND SIZE TO CUT FOR 24 SETTING TRIANGLES	QTY, SHAPE, AND SIZE TO CUT FOR 24 SETTING TRIANGLES	QTY OF SHAPE IN 1 SETTING TRIANGLE
LIGHT (L)	⅝ yard	4 strips 3½″ × WOF	72 triangles 3½″ (page 116)	3
MEDIUM (M)	1 yard	8 strips 3¼″ × WOF	72 diamonds 3¼″ (page 117)	3

Piecing

Review General Information for Making Blocks (page 32). Seam allowances are ¼″ unless otherwise noted. Follow the arrows for pressing directions.

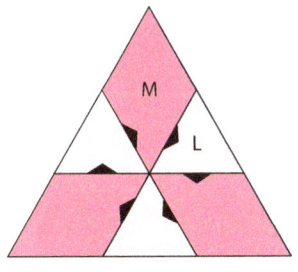

Chestnut setting triangle piecing

1. Using 3 M diamonds and 3 L triangles, arrange 1 setting triangle.

2. Sew 2 M diamonds to 1 L triangle. Sew 2 L triangles to 1 M diamond.

3. Join the units to complete 1 setting triangle.

4. Make 24 or as many as are needed for the chosen quilt design.

Chestnut setting triangle in a quilt design

DARLING

With small diamonds radiating from the center, a little extra color can be sprinkled throughout the quilt. See *Galaxy of Stars* (page 81), *Poinsettia* (page 81), and *Scarlet Knight* (page 95) for examples of this setting triangle in action.

Finished Darling setting triangle: 8¼″

YARDAGE AND CUTTING

Cut the strips and corresponding shapes using the instructions on the pages noted in the table. Refer to Figuring Yardage for Setting Triangles (page 30) for other quantities.

FABRIC	YDG FOR 24 SETTING TRIANGLES	STRIP QTY AND SIZE TO CUT FOR 24 SETTING TRIANGLES	QTY, SHAPE, AND SIZE TO CUT FOR 24 SETTING TRIANGLES	QTY OF SHAPE IN 1 SETTING TRIANGLE
LIGHT (L)	¾ yard	10 strips 2⅛″ × WOF	288 triangles 2⅛″ (page 116)	12
MEDIUM (M)	⅝ yard	4 strips 3½″ × WOF	72 triangles 3½″ (page 116)	3
DARK (D)	⅝ yard	9 strips 1⅞″ × WOF	144 diamonds 1⅞″ (page 117)	6

Piecing

Review General Information for Making Blocks (page 32). Seam allowances are ¼″ unless otherwise noted. Follow the arrows for pressing directions.

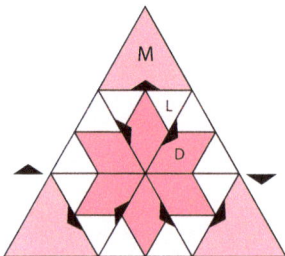

Darling setting triangle piecing

Darling setting triangle in a quilt design

1. Using 12 L triangles, 3 M triangles, and 6 D diamonds, arrange 1 setting triangle.

2. Sew 2 L triangles to 1 D diamond. Make 6 of these units.

3. Sew the units into groups of 3 to make half-hexagons. Then sew the center seam.

4. Sew 3 M triangles on alternating sides to complete 1 setting triangle.

5. Make as many as are needed for the chosen quilt design.

SERENDIPITY

This basic setting triangle is made using a hexagon of repeat-fabric triangles with three corner triangles added. It is the most common design used in between the block designs. The yardage for the repeat fabric has already been included in the block yardages. Here are just a few examples of quilts using this setting triangle: *Many Winds* (page 76), *Flint* (page 80), *Poinsettia* (page 81), *Jungle Fever* (page 84), *Button* (page 88), *Dainty* (page 88), and *Moonglow* (page 89).

Finished Serendipity setting triangle: 8¼″

YARDAGE AND CUTTING

Cut the strips and corresponding shapes using the instructions on the pages noted in the table. Refer to Figuring Yardage for Setting Triangles (page 30) for other quantities.

FABRIC	YDG FOR 24 SETTING TRIANGLES	STRIP QTY AND SIZE TO CUT FOR 24 SETTING TRIANGLES	QTY, SHAPE, AND SIZE TO CUT FOR 24 SETTING TRIANGLES	QTY OF SHAPE IN 1 SETTING TRIANGLE
REPEAT (R)	Included in block design	3 stacked strip sets 3½″ × 20″	24 triangle sets 3½″ (page 116)	1 set of 6
LIGHT (L)	⅝ yard	4 strips 3½″ × WOF	72 triangles 3½″ (page 116)	3

Piecing

Review General Information for Making Blocks (page 32). Seam allowances are ¼″ unless otherwise noted. Follow the arrows for pressing directions.

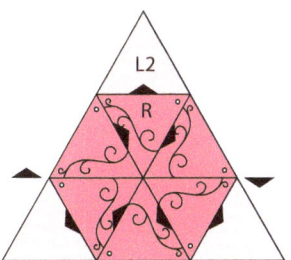

Serendipity setting triangle piecing

1. Determine the best selection of a 3½″ R triangle set (see Cutting the Strips, page 18). After the shapes are cut, refer to Design Possibilities (page 18) for ideas on how the shapes can be rotated for different looks. When you've determined the best look for each set of shapes, mark the center so you can piece them together appropriately.

2. Using 1 repeat triangle set and 3 L triangles, arrange 1 setting triangle.

3. Sew the R triangles into 2 groups of 3 to make half-hexagons. Sew the center seam to complete the hexagon.

4. Add the 3 L triangles on alternating corners.

5. Make as many as are needed for the chosen quilt design.

Serendipity setting triangle in a quilt design

Setting Triangle Designs 105

SHAMROCK

Made with at least two different fabrics, the shamrock is formed by the three triangles floating in the center. Use three or more fabrics to add extra sparkle. See *Tigerstripe* (page 77) for an example of this fun design.

Finished Shamrock setting triangle: 8¼″

YARDAGE AND CUTTING

Cut the strips and corresponding shapes using the instructions on the pages noted in the table. Refer to Figuring Yardage for Setting Triangles (page 30) for other quantities.

FABRIC	YDG FOR 24 SETTING TRIANGLES	STRIP QTY AND SIZE TO CUT FOR 24 SETTING TRIANGLES	QTY, SHAPE, AND SIZE TO CUT FOR 24 SETTING TRIANGLES	QTY OF SHAPE IN 1 SETTING TRIANGLE
LIGHT (L)	1 yard	8 strips 3½″ × WOF	144 triangles 3½″ (page 116)	6
MEDIUM (M)	⅝ yard	4 strips 3½″ × WOF	72 triangles 3½″ (page 116)	3

Piecing

Review General Information for Making Blocks (page 32). Seam allowances are ¼″ unless otherwise noted. Follow the arrows for pressing directions.

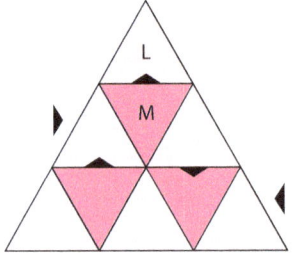

Shamrock setting triangle piecing

1. Using 6 L triangles and 3 M triangles, arrange 1 setting triangle.

2. Sew 2 L triangles to 1 M triangle to make the middle unit.

3. Sew 3 L triangles to 2 M triangles to make the lower unit.

4. Join the middle and lower units. Add 1 L triangle to the top to complete 1 setting triangle.

5. Make as many as are needed for the chosen quilt design.

Shamrock setting triangle in a quilt design

SMILE

This basic setting is a hexagon with three corner triangles added. The central shape is perfect for quilting and embroidery design space. No repeats are used with this setting triangle, so it can be used when there is not enough repeat fabric. For examples, see *Butterflies in My Garden* (page 24), *Park Place* (variation) (page 78), and *Dewdrops* (page 89).

Finished Smile setting triangle: 8¼″

YARDAGE AND CUTTING

Cut the strips and corresponding shapes using the instructions on the pages noted in the table. Refer to Figuring Yardage for Setting Triangles (page 30) for other quantities.

FABRIC	YDG FOR 24 SETTING TRIANGLES	STRIP QTY AND SIZE TO CUT FOR 24 SETTING TRIANGLES	QTY, SHAPE, AND SIZE TO CUT FOR 24 SETTING TRIANGLES	QTY OF SHAPE IN 1 SETTING TRIANGLE
MEDIUM (M)	1 yard	5 strips 6″ × WOF	24 hexagons 6″ (page 121)	1
LIGHT (L)	⅝ yard	4 strips 3½″ × WOF	72 triangles 3½″ (page 116)	3

Piecing

Review General Information for Making Blocks (page 32). Seam allowances are ¼″ unless otherwise noted. Follow the arrows for pressing directions.

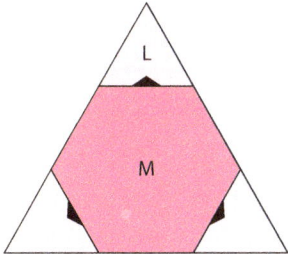

Smile setting triangle piecing

1. Using 1 M hexagon and 3 L triangles, arrange 1 setting triangle.

2. Sew the 3 L triangles on alternating corners of the M hexagon.

3. Make as many as are needed for the chosen quilt design.

Smile setting triangle in a quilt design

STARBURST

The diamonds radiate in this design. Bright and bold or soft and subtle, this setting unit joins the most intricate of quilt designs. To see how this pieced triangle adds a burst of energy to the design, see *Protect and Serve* (page 72), *A Child's Christmas* (page 84), *Mood Indigo* (page 85), and *Sunshine & Shadow* (page 92).

Finished Starburst setting triangle: 8¼″

YARDAGE AND CUTTING

Cut the strips and corresponding shapes using the instructions on the pages noted in the table. Refer to Figuring Yardage for Setting Triangles (page 30) for other quantities.

FABRIC	YDG FOR 24 SETTING TRIANGLES	STRIP QTY AND SIZE TO CUT FOR 24 SETTING TRIANGLES	QTY, SHAPE, AND SIZE TO CUT FOR 24 SETTING TRIANGLES	QTY OF SHAPE IN 1 SETTING TRIANGLE
LIGHT (L)	1 yard	5 strips 2⅛″ × WOF	144 triangles 2⅛″ (page 116)	6
		9 strips 1⅞″ × WOF	144 diamonds 1⅞″ (page 117)	6
DARK 1 (D1)	⅝ yard	9 strips 1⅞″ × WOF	144 diamonds 1⅞″ (page 117)	6
DARK 2 (D2)	½ yard	5 strips 1⅞″ × WOF	72 diamonds 1⅞″ (page 117)	3

Starburst setting triangle in a quilt design

Piecing

Review General Information for Making Blocks (page 32). Seam allowances are ¼″ unless otherwise noted. Follow the arrows for pressing directions.

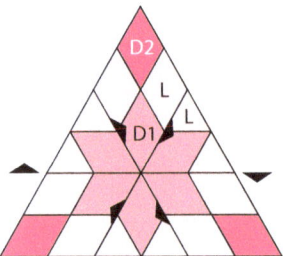

Starburst setting triangle piecing

1. Using 6 L triangles, 6 L diamonds, 6 D1 diamonds, and 3 D2 diamonds, arrange 1 setting triangle.

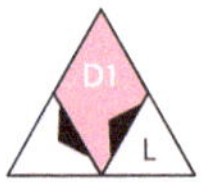

Starburst triangle unit piecing

2. Sew 2 L triangles to 1 D1 diamond. Make 3 of this triangle unit.

Starburst diamond unit piecing

3. Sew 2 L diamonds, 1 D1 diamond, and 1 D2 diamond together to make a four-patch. Make 3 of this diamond unit.

4. Sew 2 triangle units to the sides of 1 diamond unit to make the upper unit.

5. Sew 2 diamond units to the sides of 1 triangle unit to make the lower unit.

6. Join the upper and lower units to complete 1 setting triangle.

7. Make as many as are needed for the chosen quilt design.

BORDER DESIGNS

Fitting the Pieced Borders to the Quilt

The challenge with pieced borders in general is making the border lengths fit the center portion and meet at the corners exactly with the design elements. Unlike squares that have both sides the same length, 60° designs have a length and width that are not equal. Below are some guidelines and different methods for making pieced borders fit a quilt.

Option 1

Place your pieced units as desired and fill in the gaps with background fabric. This may mean using one less unit to make a shorter border and adding pieces to the ends. For examples, see *Button* (page 88) and *Dewdrops* (page 89). The inside border in *Flint* (page 80) and the outer border in *Waving Flags* (page 84) get around the corner by extending the background at the ends.

Option 2

When a pieced border as given will not fit, apply inner filler borders first. This way you can add on what you need to make the pieced borders fit. Follow these steps:

1. Divide the quilt length by the border unit length.

2. Round up for the number of units in the side borders.

3. Subtract the quilt length from the pieced border length. Divide by 2. This is the finished strip width to add at the top and bottom of the quilt. If this is too narrow, add 1 more unit to the length and refigure this strip width. Add ½″ for seam allowance.

4. Repeat this process for the quilt width. The added strip widths are likely not the same. See *Two-Sided Serendipity Sampler* (page 83), *Jungle Fever* (page 84), and *Badge* (page 87) for examples of this method.

Figuring Yardage for Pieced Borders

Each border design has its own table with the shapes, their sizes, and the quantity needed per unit. Once the number of units is known (56 units for this example), the yardage can be determined from the table.

Light fabric half-diamond:
1. Multiply the number of units by the quantity of the shape needed per unit: 56 × 2 = 112.

2. Divide this total number of shapes by the number of half-diamonds per 2⅛″ × WOF strip, and round up. 112 ÷ 9 = 12.4, therefore 13 strips are needed.

3. Multiply the number of strips by the width of the strip. Add extra for straightening or a miscut. 13 × 2⅛″ = 27⅝″ + 2⅛″ + 3″ = 32¾″ (Round up to 1 yard.)

Medium fabric diamond:

Following the instructions in Steps 1–3 for the light fabric, do the calculations for the medium fabric.

1. 56 units × 1 shape per unit = 56

2. 56 ÷ 10 long diamonds per 3¼″ × WOF strip = 5.6, therefore 6 strips

3. 6 strips × 3¼″ = 19½″, 19½″ + 3¼″ + 3″ = 25.75″ (Round up to ¾ yard.)

Example table

FABRIC	SHAPE AND SIZE	QTY PER STRIP	QTY FOR 1 UNIT
LIGHT (L)	2⅛″ half-diamond (page 122)	9 / 40″	2
MEDIUM (M)	3¼″ diamond (page 122)	10 / 40″	1

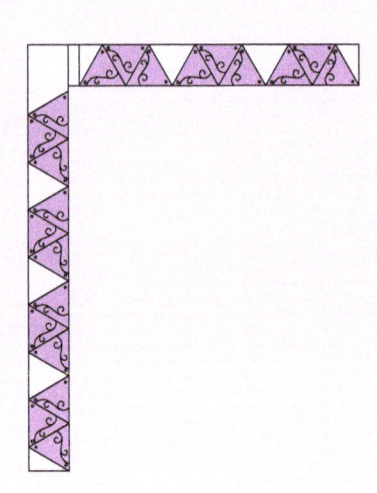

BUNTING

The sizes shown in the diagram are *finished* sizes. Using these numbers, determine how many units are needed for the top and bottom borders and for the side borders, following the directions in Fitting the Pieced Borders to the Quilt (page 109). Use the chart below to determine how much fabric is required for your design. See the example in Figuring Yardage for Pieced Borders (page 109). For an example of this border design, see *Waving Flags* (page 84).

Finished Bunting border unit: 2¾″ × 6⅜″

YARDAGE AND CUTTING

Cut and piece the border units using the table and the diagrams below.

FABRIC	SHAPE AND SIZE	QTY PER STRIP	QTY FOR 1 UNIT
REPEAT (R) (A set is 6 layers.)	3½″ triangle (page 116)	8 / 20″	½ of set
LIGHT (L)	3½″ triangle (page 116)	18 / 40″	1 = 4 total for border ends

1. If needed, add inner filler borders to the quilt top. See Fitting the Pieced Borders to the Quilt, Option 2 (page 109), or use Option 1, filling the gaps with background fabric.

2. Using 3 triangles from an R set and 1 L triangle, sew together a 4-piece unit, with the L triangle consistently on the same side of the repeat fabric.

3. Join these together on the diagonal seams.

4. Use background rectangles to extend the borders as needed. Measure the quilt top and square the ends of one set of borders. Sew these 2 borders onto the quilt.

5. Measure the other direction and trim the second set of borders to that length. Join these borders to complete this part of the quilt. Add more borders as desired.

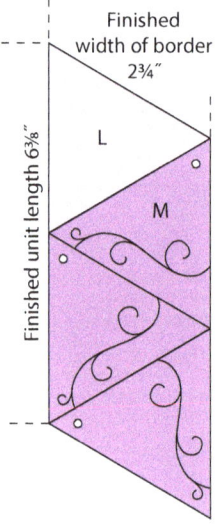

Bunting border piecing

DOUBLE DIAMOND

The sizes shown in the diagram are *finished* sizes. Using these numbers, determine how many units are needed for the top and bottom borders and for the side borders, following the directions in Fitting the Pieced Borders to the Quilt (page 109). Use the chart below to determine how much fabric is required for your design. See the example in Figuring Yardage for Pieced Borders (page 109). For an example of this border, see *Tigerstripe* (page 77).

Finished Double Diamond border unit: 3⅛″ × 5½″

YARDAGE AND CUTTING

Cut and piece the border units using the table and the diagrams below.

FABRIC	SHAPE AND SIZE	QTY PER STRIP	QTY FOR 1 UNIT
LIGHT (L)	2⅛″ strip, 1 per strip set, 3½″ strip-pieced triangle (page 116)	18 / 40″	2
MEDIUM (M)	1⅞″ strips, 2 per strip set, 3½″ strip-pieced triangle (page 116)		
	2⅛″ half-diamond (page 122)	9 / 40″	2
DARK (D)	1 strip 2⅜″, subcut into 4 rectangles 2⅜″ × 4⅛″	9 / 40″	Total for 4 borders: 8 left triangle halves (page 115)

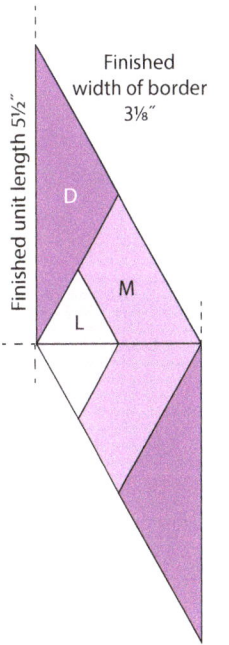

Double Diamond border piecing

1. If needed, add inner filler borders to the quilt top. See Fitting the Pieced Borders to the Quilt, Option 2 (page 109).

2. Sew 2 L-M strip-pieced triangles together, matching the light triangles to create a diamond.

3. Sew 2 D half-diamonds to the diamond.

4. Join these together on the diagonal seams.

5. In *Tigerstripe* (page 77), these borders matched the length of the sides. The top and bottom were made to extend as far as possible using whole units, and a strip of background fabric was added to complete the length.

RICKRACK

The sizes shown in the diagram are *finished* sizes. Using these numbers, determine how many units are needed for the top and bottom borders and for the side borders, following the directions in Fitting the Pieced Borders to the Quilt (page 109). Also, since this is a long unit that overlaps, plan on four extra units for each border. Once you know how many units you will need, add sixteen total for the ends of the borders. Use the chart below to determine how much fabric is required for your design. See the example in Figuring Yardage for Pieced Borders (page 109). For an example of this border, see *Scrap Star* (page 94).

Finished Rickrack border unit: 4¾″ × 5½″

YARDAGE AND CUTTING

Cut and piece the border units using the table and the diagrams below.

FABRIC	SHAPE AND SIZE	QTY PER STRIP	QTY FOR 1 UNIT
LIGHT (L)	2⅛″ half-diamond (page 122)	9 / 40″	2
MEDIUM (M)	6″ long diamond from 3¼″ strip (page 118)	6 / 40″	1

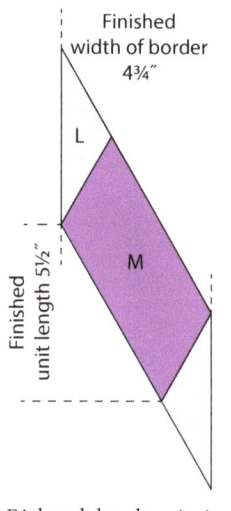

Rickrack border piecing

1. If needed, add inner filler borders to quilt top. See Fitting the Pieced Borders to the Quilt, Option 2 (page 109).

2. Sew 1 half-diamond to each short side of the long diamond.

3. Join these together on the diagonal seams.

4. In the quilt *Scrap Star* (page 94), Sara used these borders only on the sides of the quilt. If using this border on all 4 sides, use a plain square at the corners for the easiest method to finish the design.

TRIPLE TRIANGLE

The sizes shown in the diagram are *finished* sizes. Using these numbers, determine how many units are needed for the top and bottom borders and for the side borders, following the directions in Fitting the Pieced Borders to the Quilt (page 109). Use the chart below to determine how much fabric is required for your design. See the example in Figuring Yardage for Pieced Borders (page 109). For an example of this border, see *Shimmer* (page 82).

Finished Triple Triangle border unit: 2¾″ × 3⅛″

YARDAGE AND CUTTING

Cut and piece the border units using the table and the diagrams below.

FABRIC	SHAPE AND SIZE	QTY PER STRIP	QTY FOR 1 UNIT
LIGHT (L)	2⅛″ triangle (page 116)	31 / 40″	3
DARK (D)	2⅛″ triangle (page 116)	31 / 40″	1
	3½″ triangle (page 116)	18 / 40″	1

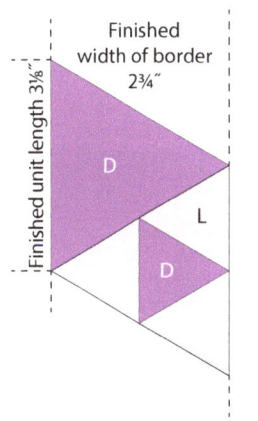

Triple Triangle border piecing

1. If needed, add inner filler borders to quilt top. See Fitting the Pieced Borders to the Quilt, Option 2 (page 109).

2. Sew 3 L 2⅛″ triangles to 1 D 2⅛″ triangle.

3. Add 1 D 3½″ triangle to one side.

4. Join these together on the diagonal seams. End with 3½″ D triangles on each end.

5. Trim the ends square. Attach squares to the second pair of borders and join to the quilt top.

A variation on this border, called Simple Triangles, uses full triangles in place of the pieced unit. Use the yardage in the Triple Triangles for the 3½″ D triangles to determine what is needed for this design. See *Badge* (page 87).

Border Designs

ZIGZAG

The sizes shown in the diagram are *finished* sizes. Using these numbers, determine how many units are needed for the top and bottom borders and for the side borders, following the directions in Fitting the Pieced Borders to the Quilt (page 109). Use the chart below to determine how much fabric is required for your design. See the example in Figuring Yardage for Pieced Borders (page 109). For an example of this border see, *Two-Sided Serendipity Sampler* (page 83).

Finished Zigzag border unit: 2¾″ × 6⅜″

YARDAGE AND CUTTING

Cut and piece the border units using the table and the diagrams below.

FABRIC	SHAPE AND SIZE	QTY PER STRIP	QTY FOR 1 UNIT
LIGHT (L)	3½″ triangle (page 116)	18 / 40″	2
	2⅜″ strip, subcut into 4 rectangles 2⅜ × 4⅛	8 / 40″	2 triangle halves (page 115) per border. Cut left or right as needed.
DARK (D)	1⅞″ strip, subcut into 3¼″ long diamonds (page 118)	10 / 40″	2 (1 L and 1 R)

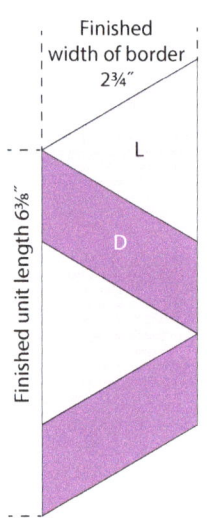

Zigzag border piecing

1. If needed, add inner filler borders to quilt top. See Fitting the Pieced Borders to the Quilt, Option 2 (page 109).

2. For 1 unit, sew 2 D long diamonds—1 left and 1 right—alternating with 2 L triangles, as shown.

3. Join these units together. Partial units may be needed to fit the border to the quilt. End each border with 1 left and 1 right triangle half.

4. Add the side borders. Sew the squares to the ends of the top and bottom borders. Add the top and bottom borders to complete the quilt.

CUTTING SHAPES

These instructions use the Clearview Triangle or Clearview Super 60° ruler (see Tools, page 10). If you choose to work with patterns instead, see Patterns (page 124). The patterns can also be used to verify that what you have cut is correct. This provides extra confidence in your project.

Sara and Marci have different methods for working with dog-ears when cutting shapes. Sara leaves them on for alignment when completing the blocks; Marci trims them off when cutting the shapes to make piecing faster at the sewing machine. Try each method and see which one fits your style. Photos are provided throughout the cutting instructions, indicating which points to trim using the Corner Cut 60—2-in-1 Sewing Tool (by C&T Publishing).

Triangle Halves

Left Halves

Use a rectangle cut to the appropriate size. (For this example, we used 3¾″ × 6½″.) Place the rectangle so that the shorter sides are horizontal. Place the ruler, point up, at the upper left corner, and align a centerline to the rectangle's left edge. Do not twist the ruler to match the corners. Keep the 60° angle by aligning the ruler with the edges of the rectangle. Cut along the ruler's right edge. If desired, trim off the dog-ears for faster sewing.

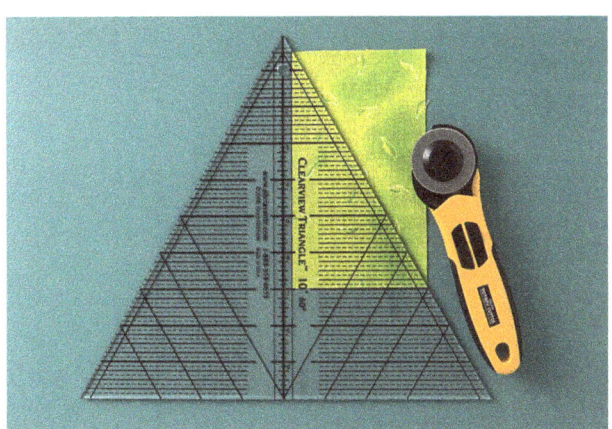

Right Halves

Use a rectangle cut to the appropriate size. (For this example, we used 3¾″ × 6½″.) Arrange the rectangle and ruler as described in Left Halves (at left), but this time have the ruler point down at the lower left corner. Cut along the ruler's right edge. If desired, trim off the dog-ears for faster sewing.

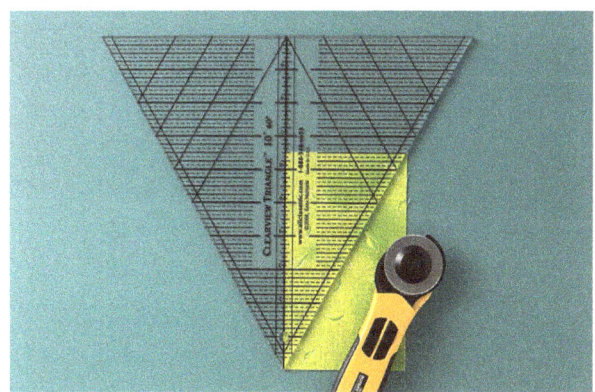

Triangles

1. Cut a strip to the appropriate width for your project. (For this example, we used a 3″ strip.) At the right end of this strip, place the ruler with a point up and the ruler line aligned with the strip's lower edge. Cut along the ruler's right edge.

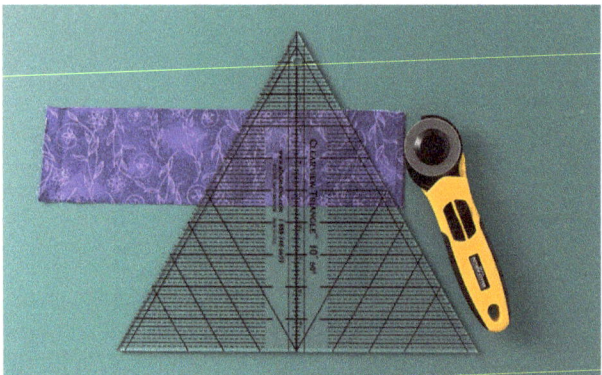

2. Turn the strip so that the angled end is to the left. With the ruler's top point down and the ruler's left edge at the left end of the strip, align the triangle size line (this is the same as the strip width: 3″) along the top of the strip. Cut along the ruler's right edge.

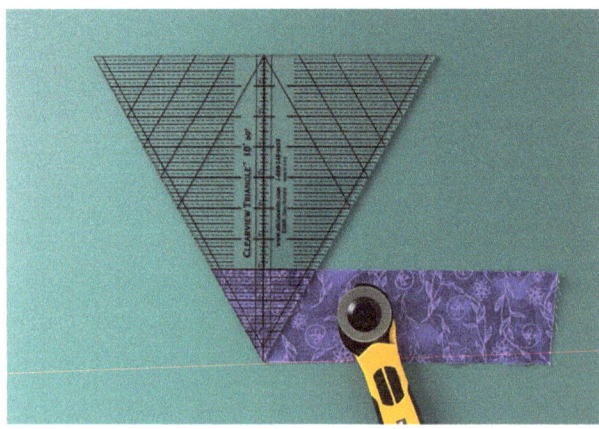

3. Rotate the ruler so that the top point is up and the triangle size line is now along the bottom of the strip. Cut. Repeat Steps 2 and 3 until you have the required number of triangles for your project.

4. To make sewing easier and faster at the machine, trim off the dog-ears at each corner before you remove the pieces from the mat.

Strip-Pieced Triangles

There are 2 fabrics in each triangle. To make the sewing and cutting more efficient, 3 strips are sewn together, slices are cut, and then the triangles are cut. Follow these steps.

1. Sew the narrower strip on each side of the wider strip. Cut a 60° angle at the end of the strip set. See Triangles, Step 1 (at left).

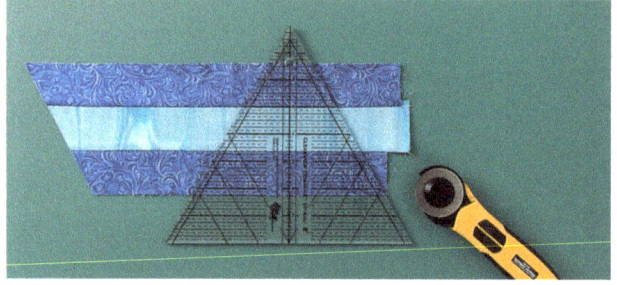

2. Turn the strip set around and cut slices of the appropriate size, measuring from the bottom of the ruler (3½″ is shown).

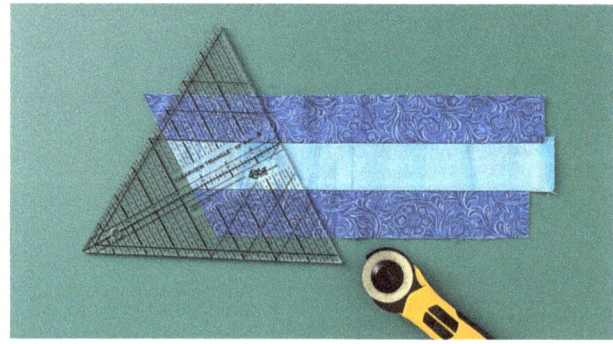

3. Cut 2 triangles of the given size from each slice.

4. *Optional:* Trim the dog-ears from the 3 corners to make sewing easier and faster.

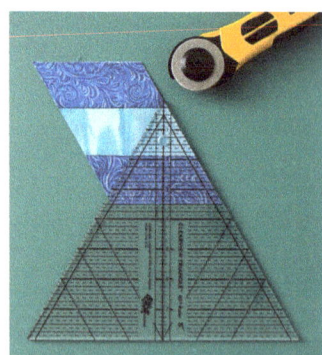

Diamonds

1. Cut a strip the appropriate width for your project. (For this example, we use a 3″ strip.) At the right end of the strip, place the ruler with one side or line aligned with the strip's lower edge. Cut along the ruler's right edge to yield a 60° angle.

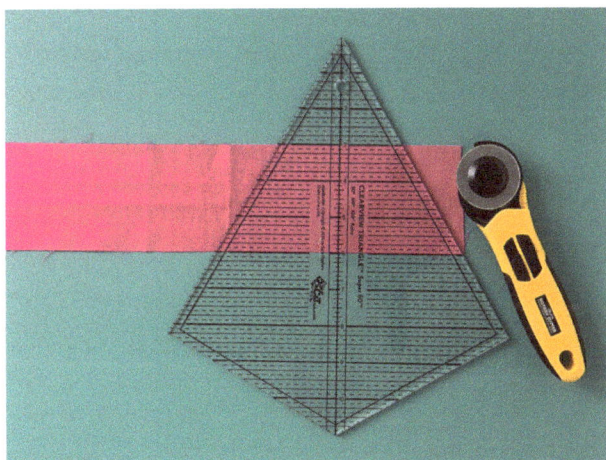

2. Turn the strip with the angled end to the left.

If using the Clearview Triangle ruler: Place the ruler at the left end of the strip so that the top point is at the lower left. To make the diamond the same width as the strip, align the edge of the fabric with the line measured from the bottom of the ruler for your chosen size. (The example shown is a 3″ diamond.) Cut along the ruler's right edge.

If using the Clearview Super 60° ruler: Place the ruler with the top point up so that the ruler's edge is at the lower left corner and the ruler line for your chosen diamond size is at the bottom edge of the strip. (The example shown is a 3″ diamond.) Cut *only* on the ruler's right edge.

3. *Optional:* Trim off the dog-ears to make sewing easier and faster.

Long Diamonds

Left

1. Cut a strip to the appropriate width for your project. Place the ruler with a point facing up and the ¼" line aligned with the lower edge of the strip. Cut along the ruler's right edge.

Using Clearview Triangle ruler

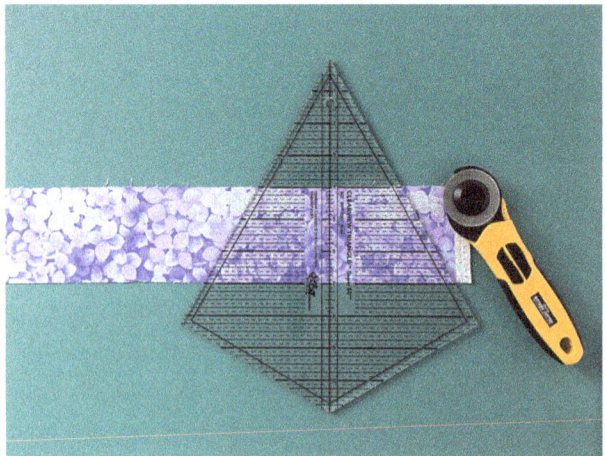

Using Clearview Super 60° ruler

2. Turn the strip with the angled end to the left. Note how this cut end angles to the left.

If using the Clearview Triangle ruler: Place the ruler at the left end of the strip so that the top point is at the lower left and the ¼" line is along the bottom of the strip. Align the appropriate ruler line, measured from the bottom of the ruler, with the cut end of the strip. (In the example shown, the measurement is 6".) Cut the long diamond. Repeat this process to make the necessary number of left long diamonds.

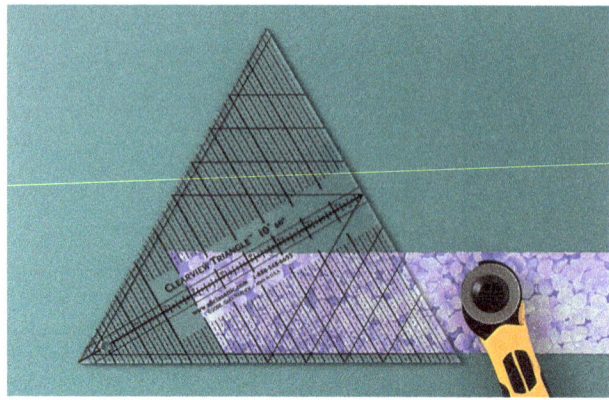

If using the Clearview Super 60° ruler: Place the ruler at the left end of the strip with the top point up. Align the appropriate ruler line, measured from the top of the ruler, with the bottom edge of the strip. (In the example shown, the measurement is 6".) Also align the ruler's left edge to match the lower left corner of the strip. Make the cut only on the strip's right edge. Repeat this process to make the necessary number of left long diamonds.

3. *Optional:* Trim off the dog-ears to make sewing easier and faster.

118   STACK & CUT Hexagon Quilts

Right

1. Cut a strip to the appropriate width for your project. At the right end of the strip, place the ruler with a point facing down and the ¼″ line aligned with the upper edge of the strip. Cut along the ruler's right edge.

Using Clearview Triangle ruler

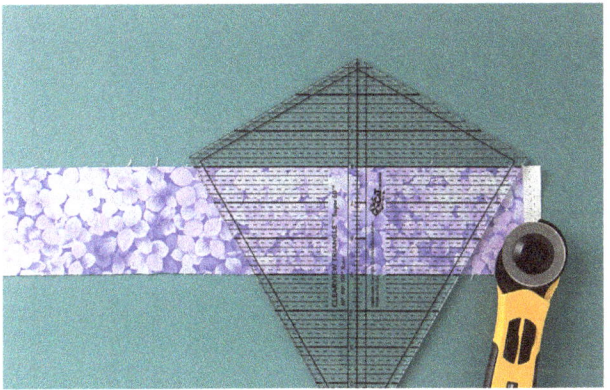

Using Clearview Super 60° ruler

2. Turn the strip with the angled end to the left. Note how this cut end angles to the right.

If using the Clearview Triangle ruler: Place the ruler at the left end of the strip so that the top point is at the upper left and the ¼″ line is along the top of the strip. Align the appropriate ruler line, measured from the bottom of the ruler, with the cut end of the strip. (In the example shown, the measurement is 6″.) Cut the long diamond. Repeat this process to make the necessary number of right long diamonds.

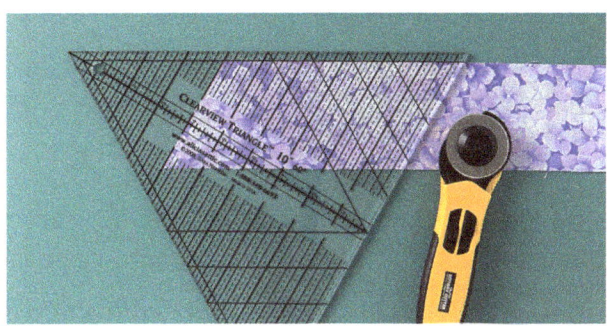

If using the Clearview Super 60° ruler: Place the ruler at the left end of the strip with the top point down. Align the appropriate ruler line (measured from the top of the ruler) with the top edge of the strip. Also align the ruler's left edge to match the upper left corner of the strip. Make the cut only on the strip's right edge. Repeat this process to make the necessary number of right long diamonds.

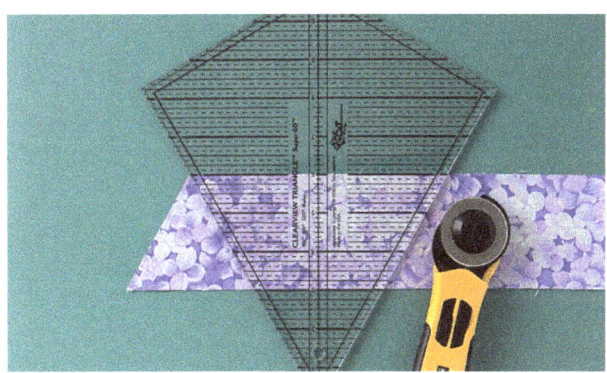

3. *Optional:* Trim off the dog-ears to make sewing easier and faster.

tip Stacking Left and Right Long Diamonds
Cut both left and right long diamonds at the same time by stacking the strips. Place the right fabric wrong side up, and then stack the left fabric on top, right side up. After arranging the stack, follow the instructions for cutting left long diamonds (previous page).

Strip-Pieced Diamonds

Sew 2 strips together to make a strip set. Press the seams to one side.

Left

1. At the right end of the strip set, place the ruler so that the point is up and a ¼" line is aligned with the seam and/or the lower edge of the strip. Cut along the ruler's right edge.

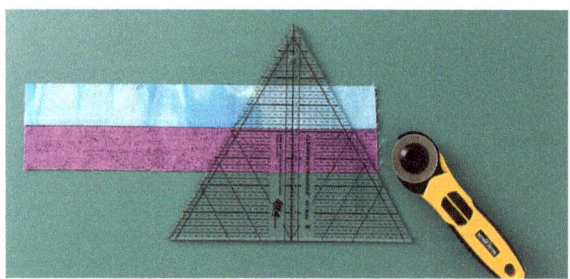

2. Turn the strip around. Place the ruler at the left end, with the top point to the lower left and the ¼" line along the bottom of the strip. Align the appropriate ruler line, measured from the bottom of the ruler, with the cut end of the strip. (In the example shown, the measurement is 1⅞".) Cut the left strip set.

If you are using the Clearview Super 60° ruler, use a regular ruler to measure and cut the widths in this step. Check the 60° angle often using the Clearview Super 60° ruler. If it does not align, repeat Step 1 to reestablish the 60° angle.

Right

1. At the right end of the strip set, place the ruler so that the point is down and a ¼" line is aligned with the seam and/or the upper edge of the strip. Cut along the ruler's right edge.

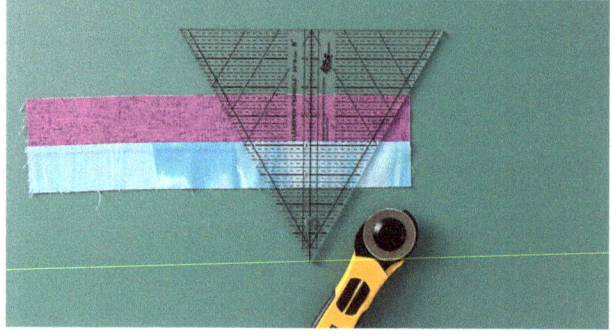

2. Turn the strip around. Place the ruler at the left end, with the top point to the upper left and a horizontal line aligned with the seam or strip edges to maintain the 60° angle. Align the appropriate ruler line, measured from the bottom of the ruler, with the cut end of the strip. (In the example shown, the measurement is 1⅞".) Cut the right strip set.

If you are using the Clearview Super 60° ruler, use a regular ruler to measure and cut the widths in this step. Check the 60° angle often using the Clearview Super 60° ruler. If it does not align, repeat Step 1 to reestablish the 60° angle.

Flat Pyramids

1. Cut a strip to the appropriate width for your project. (For this example, we used a 3″ strip.) At the right end of the strip, place the ruler so that a point is up and the lower ¼″ line is aligned with the lower edge of the strip. Cut along the ruler's right edge.

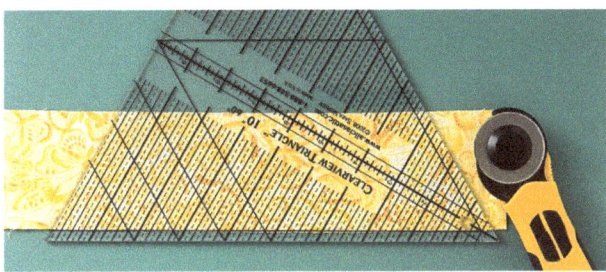

2. Turn the strip with the angled end to the left. With the point of the ruler facing down, align the flat pyramid size line along the top edge of the strip and the ruler's left edge along the left edge of the strip. (The example shows a 5″ flat pyramid cut from a 3″ strip.) Cut along the ruler's edge.

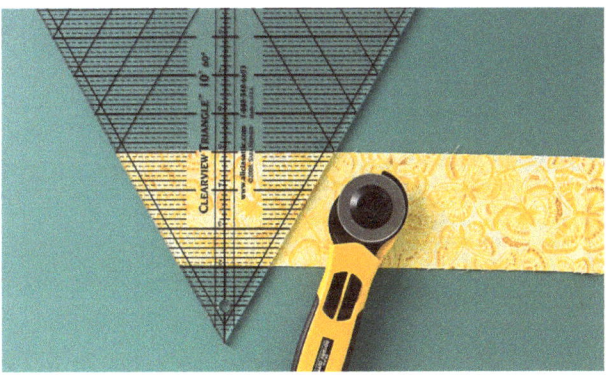

3. Rotate the ruler, align the size line along the bottom edge, and cut along the ruler's edge. Continue cutting flat pyramids until you have the number needed for your project.

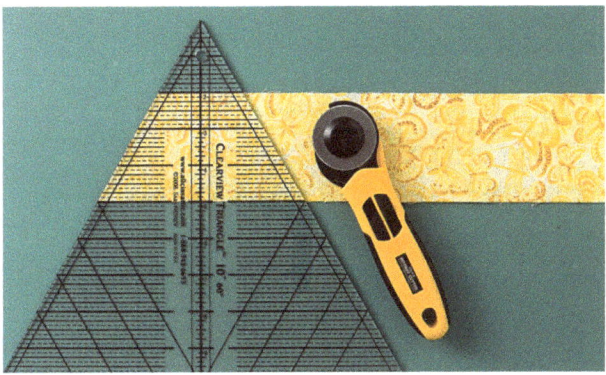

4. *Optional:* Trim off the dog-ears to make sewing easier and faster.

Gems and Hexagons

These shapes are so similar in cutting that they are shown together. Either the Clearview Triangle or the Clearview Super 60° ruler can be used for this shape.

1. Cut the designated diamond.

2a. For the gem shape, cut off one end of the diamond using the measurement given.

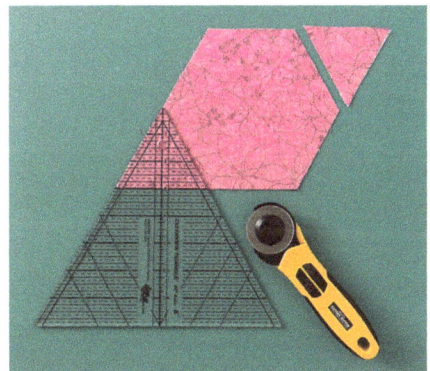

2b. For the hexagon, cut off both ends of the diamond using the measurement given.

Cutting Shapes

Matched Triangles

Whenever there is repetition in the design, you can speed piece the triangles.

1. Cut 2 strips to the appropriate width for your project. (Each project indicates the fabric combinations to sew.) With right sides together, sew these strips lengthwise down both sides. Cut triangles from this set of sewn strips (see Triangles, page 116).

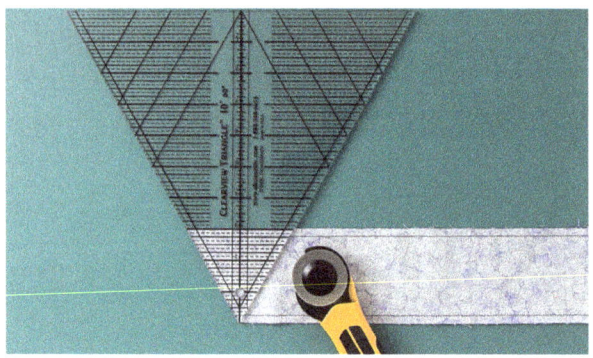

2. Pull the tips of the seamed triangles apart or trim the sewn tips using the Corner Cut 60 tool. It is not necessary to trim the other 2 corners. Press as indicated in the individual project.

Matched Half-Diamonds

Sew the 2 strips right sides together lengthwise on both sides. For single half-diamonds, do not sew the strips together and cut as shown.

Using the Clearview Super 60° Ruler

1. Place the ruler with the bottom point at the edge of the strip and the appropriate line along the other strip edge.

2. Cut on both edges of the ruler to get the first half-diamond.

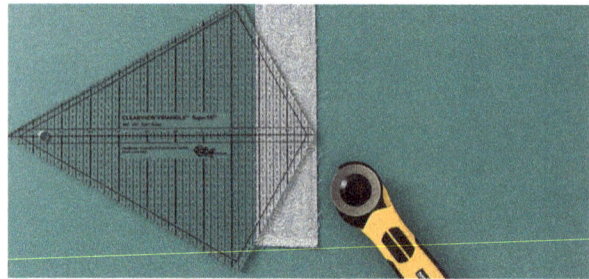

Cut half-diamond with Clearview Super 60°.

3. For subsequent cuts, alternate the placement of the Super 60° ruler.

Using the Clearview Triangle Ruler

1. Place the ruler with the centerline along the left edge of the strip and the point down.

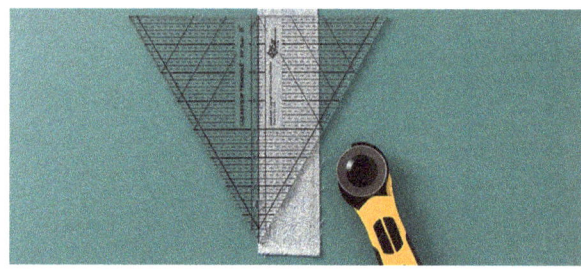

2. Trim along the ruler's right edge.

3. Rotate the ruler so the point is up and the centerline is along the left side. Slide the ruler until its right edge meets the corner at the right edge of the strip. Make the cut to get 1 matched half-diamond.

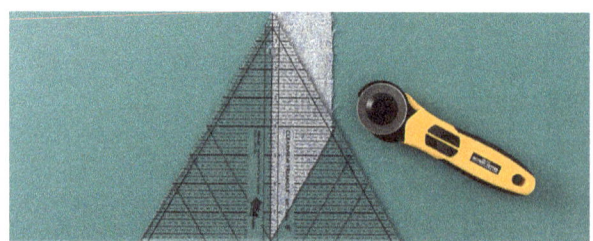

Using Either Ruler

1. Repeat Steps 2 and 3 for your chosen ruler to cut more matched half-diamonds.

2. *Optional:* Once open, trim off the dog-ears at both ends to make sewing easier and faster.

BINDING OTHER ANGLES

Several of the quilts in this book have corners that are not square, such as *Park Place* (page 75); here is how you achieve a nice miter on these corners. The seam allowance is ¼". Use your favorite width of binding strip for the ¼" binding. Marci prefers using 2"-wide strips for a precise, crisp finished binding. Sara prefers 2¼"-wide strips for a soft, flowing binding.

1. At the corner, stop at the point where the seamlines cross: ¼" away from the edges, with the needle down in the fabric. Pivot toward the corner point, and sew off the edge of the quilt.

2. Remove the quilt from the machine and turn it to work on the next side. Fold the binding back along the angled seamline. Align the binding edges with the edge of the next side of the quilt top, making a straight line.

3. Fold the binding down, in line with the corner of the top, keeping the binding edge and quilt top edge aligned.

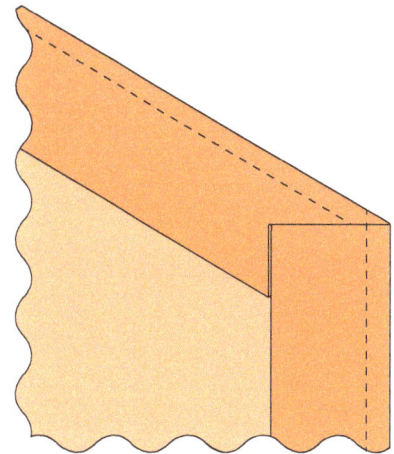

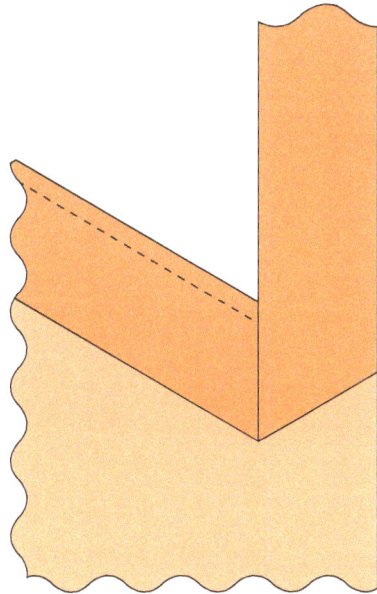

4. On the back side, fold the right side in and then the left side. This needs to be all the fabric that can wrap to the back. If there is extra left on the front, the corner will be rounded. Stitch by hand or machine. Depending on the direction the corner is sewn, the corners may need to be pinned in place.

PATTERNS

Triangle 2⅛"

Triangle 3½"

Triangle 4⅞"

Triangle 6¼"

Flat Pyramid 1⅞"-wide strip 3½" ruler line

Flat Pyramid 3¼"-wide strip 4⅞" ruler line

Half-Diamond 2⅛"-wide strip

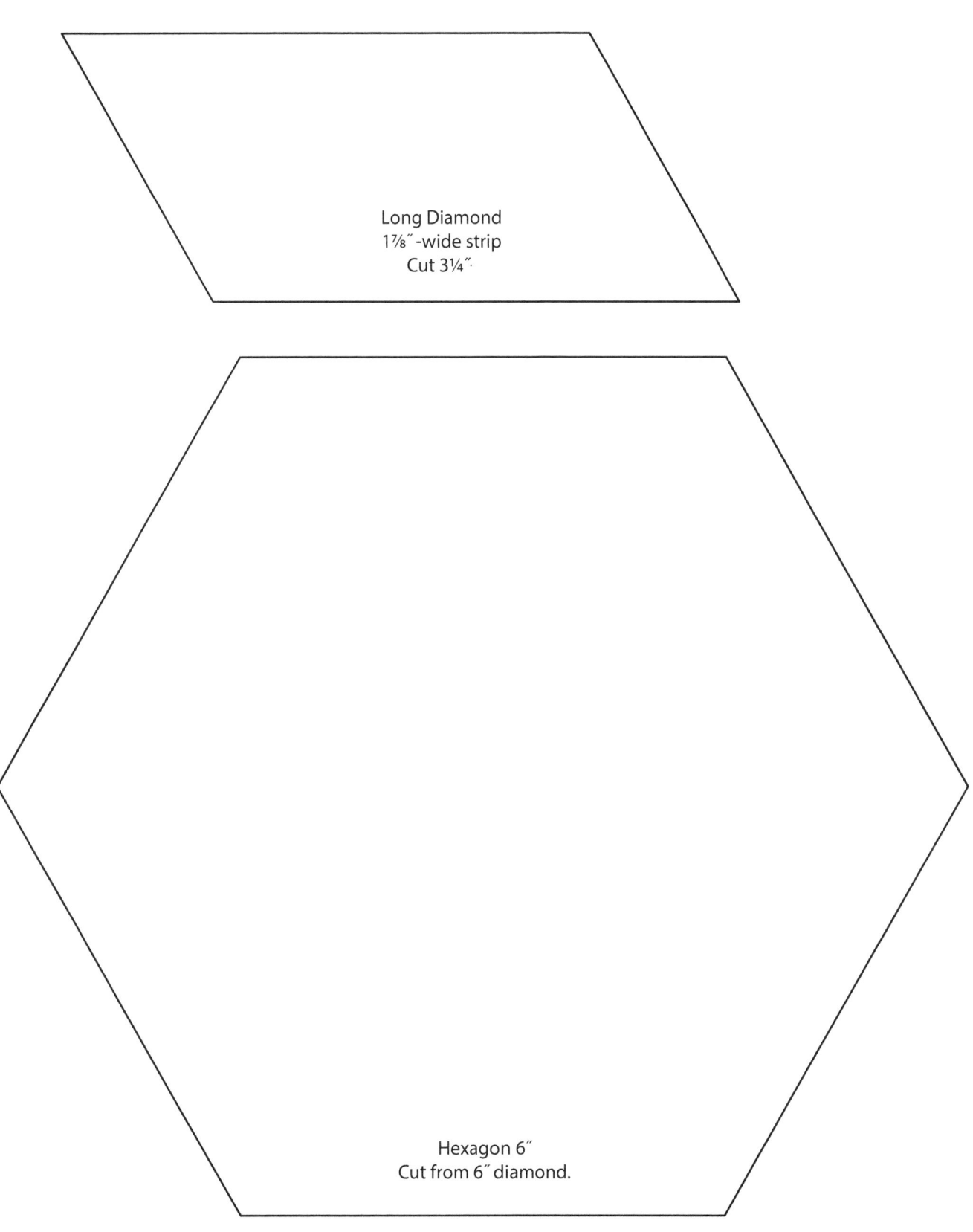

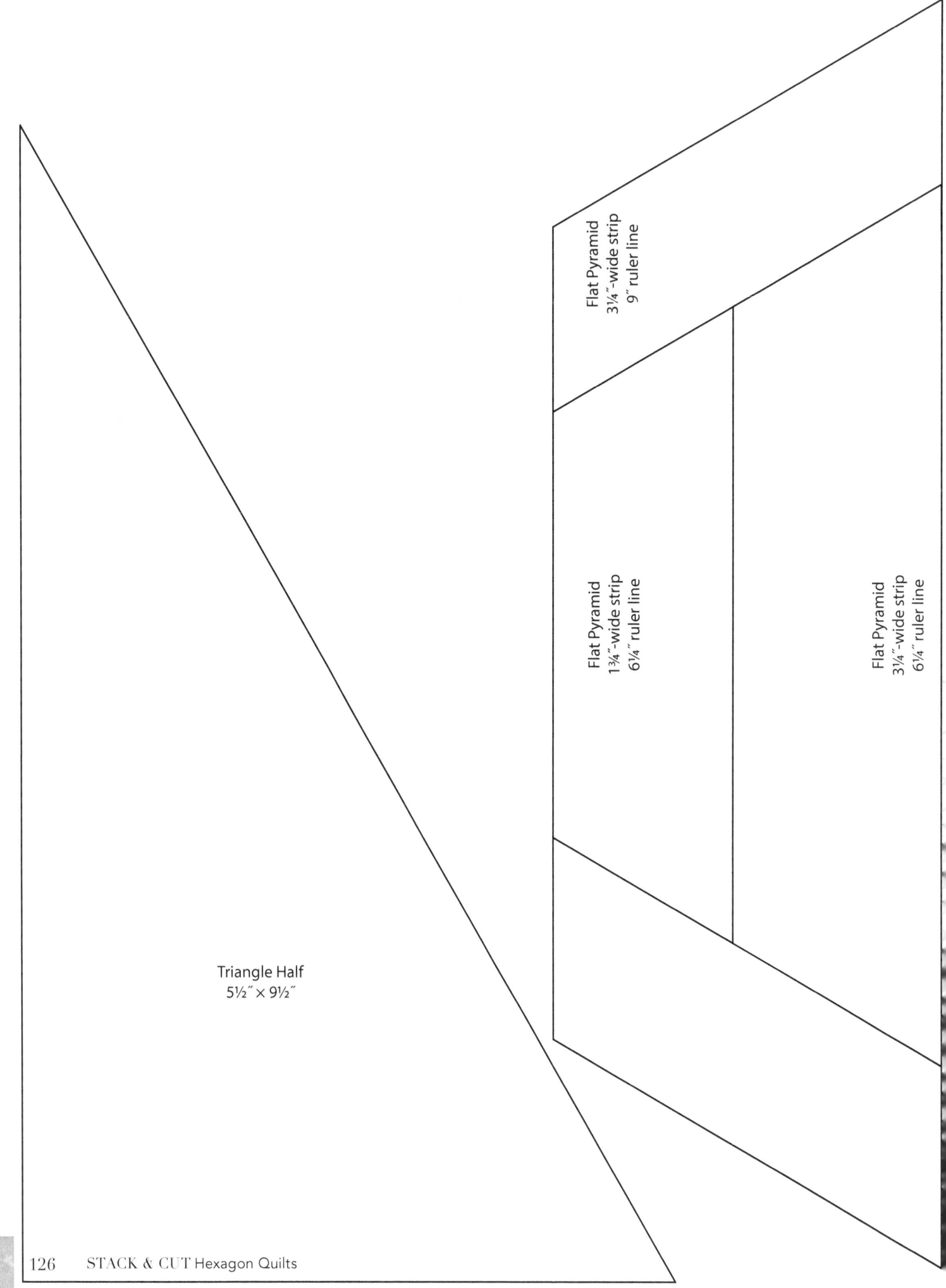

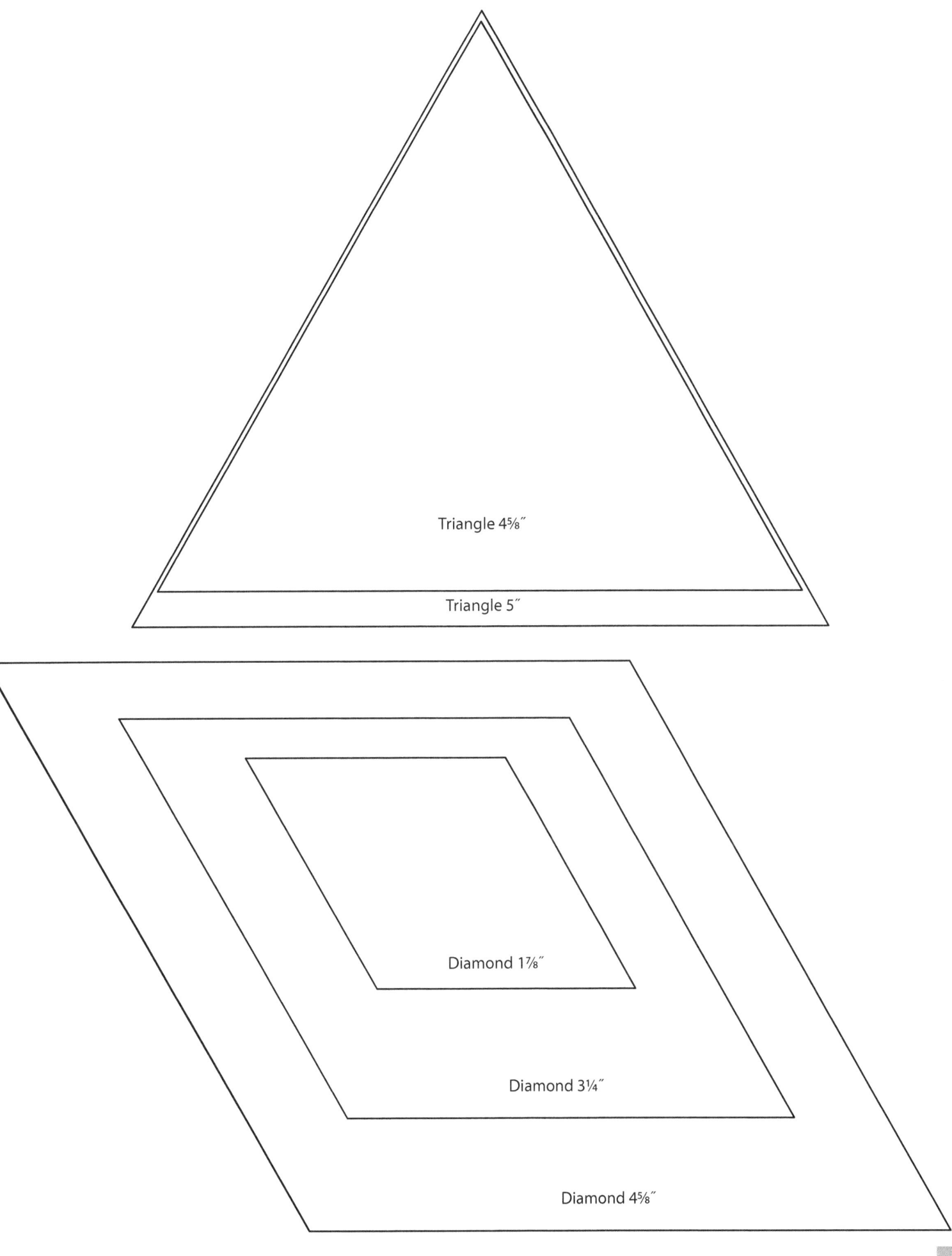

Patterns 127

ABOUT THE AUTHORS

Marci Baker

Photo by Kim Walz (Element One Studio)

Recognized internationally for her expertise in quilting, Marci enjoys sharing ideas that simplify the quilting process. A native of Dallas, Texas, Marci began teaching quilting in 1989 for her local quilting guild and shops. In 1993 she started Alicia's Attic, a company that combines her love of math and teaching with her love of quilting.

As an admirer of traditional quilts, Marci was inspired to author the Not Your Grandmother's Quilts series, which uses traditional patterns that people associate with grandmothers but simplifies the techniques. In 2006 she expanded Alicia's Attic by purchasing Clearview Triangle from Sara Nephew. Marci and Sara are collaborating on new designs and techniques, with Marci traveling and teaching under her new business name: Quilt with Marci Baker. One of her latest adventures is the Quilt with Marci Baker Certification Program. With certified instructors across the United States and Canada, her methods are readily accessible through shops, guilds, and shows.

Marci and her husband, Clint, live in Fort Collins, Colorado, where they enjoy the beautiful mountain views.

Contact Marci at marci@quiltmb.com.

Follow Marci on social media:

Website: quiltwithmarcibaker.com
(Be sure to check out her latest schedule!)

Sara Nephew

Photo by Rowland Studios

Sara is a quilt designer, author, and teacher who has developed several isometric (60°) triangle rulers. Her quilting career has taken her all over the United States, Canada, and Australia, and her quilts have been widely exhibited. Sara has been featured in magazine articles and books.

Always an artist, Sara started her career as a commercial jeweler. She began learning diamond setting as well as continuing her work with painting and cloisonné enameling. After several other careers, Sara gravitated toward quilting and found her calling.

When Sara started the Clearview Triangle business, her multifaceted quilting career took off. In 2006 she retired from the day-to-day operations of running her business and sold her company to Marci Baker of Alicia's Attic. But Sara has not stopped working, creating new quilts, or writing—as evidenced by this book!

Contact Sara at saranephew@quiltmb.com.

www.ingramcontent.com/pod-product-compliance
Lightning Source LLC
Chambersburg PA
CBHW051550220426
43671CB00024B/2991